COMING BACK

BY SAM CASTERNOVIA

About the author:

I am like you, the person across the street, the guy across the hall, the guy walking his dog.

Maybe a slight difference is the way my early years started. I watched my mom in bed dying, day after day at the age of 4, and watched my dad work day and night to keep my sister and I together was traumatic for me. I spent years waiting for the other shoe to drop, praying to be grown so I would not be defenseless, it took some of the kid out of me.

I did not know I was dyslectic as a young man, but it may have been an asset. Reading was very difficult, but I remembered everything I heard and saw. Quietly, I watched, listened and learned, and it prepared me for life. Lucky for me, because my health problems started at age 12, migraines with blackouts, bowel diseases, two life threatening cancers, a crippling bone disease, experimental surgeries, debilitating side effects from lifesaving radiation, partial vision loss, bowel blockages, many complications, follow up surgeries, long hospital stays and nerve damage in my neck, to name a few.

Today people say, "Sam, you look so good," when really what they mean is, "Damn, I thought you were dead". Going from 175lb to 125lb several times and suffering with diseases for 38 years, I get it, but hearing it often can sometimes get to you.

Well, I'm still alive and living a full life, because of my dedication and research to find the right doctor, working out with an oxygen machine, eating a restricted diet, taking supplements, staying active and maintaining a positive attitude.

I realize every person is different, as is their disease and the severity of their situation, but I'd like to share with you, collectively, what I have learned and has worked for me. Hoping you can improve your situation and live a fuller life.

My first cancer, just may have been my greatest gift in life, hence (thegiftofcancer.com)

WE GET THERE WITH HELP

I dedicate this book to those who have seen something in me, that made them help me be the best I could be.

To my father, who spent his life teaching me values and principles that saved my life, time and again.

To my wife, Lynne, who has always stood by me and inspired me to be more than I am.

To my daughter, Samantha, who set standards for our family with her battles, a gift to watch her grow.

To my sister, Irene, who in my times of need, never questioned her role, just performed.

To my best friend, Dom, always there for me, and a man who gets up in the morning for others.

To Joe Pecora and Allaire Karzon, from whom I learned to fight by using the courts and more, which brought me off the street.

To Tom Cantillon, who taught me how to write, urged me to write my story and edited this book.

To the many doctors who worked to improve my health, Dr. Robert Crozier, Dr. John Coller, Dr. Robert Dolan, Dr. Josh Garren, Dr. Thomas Read and the Lahey Clinic and Dr. Joseph Clemente.

Table of Contents

CHAPTER 1
THINKING OF YOU

The early morning hours are familiar to me, walking the floor hour after hour, sometimes through the night into the dawn. On these nights when the daylight bursts through the darkness, inviting the day's events, it is not quite the same as waking to a well-planned day of family activities or the pursuit of my goals. You see, today I am trying to get back, not ahead, back, to my well-guarded and controlled lifestyle I love so much.

2 hours into the walk and things are stable, but thoughts of the increasing discomfort in my right leg plague my thoughts of my end goal. Dealing with the pain of avascular necrosis of the right femur, I'm hoping it does not overwhelm me, does not interrupt my much needed excursion. Stopping now would only be a recipe for my intestinal blockages to take control. Funny how dehydration affects so many things. I guess it affects the fluid in the joint, normally I can walk without pain throughout my day.

The goal is simple, yet without a clearly defined path. History, gathered information and willpower are all in play, as I try to get my intestinal blockages moving again. Thinking (should I sip warm liquids as I walk, which seem to sooth me and hydrate or cold liquids that I know statistically leave the stomach faster and may offer faster relief but lack the feeling of calmness.) All the time I'm trying to keep my balance from the dehydration of the earlier vomiting, fighting the occasional episodes of blackouts from vasovagal syncope, some nights compounded by mouth and throat infections from the radiation treatments, all remnants of multiple cancers, surgeries and treatments to keep me alive.

As the morning progresses, my exhaustion and discomfort have made me more aware of every step as the pounding of my heart resonates throughout my body. I sense a slight glimpse of thankfulness though. Today, I have the privilege of walking through a large kitchen, into a 40ft. room with 14-foot ceilings, into the dining room, the front foyer, down a small hall through the rear foyer and back to my favorite room of the house, the kitchen. One big circle, that constantly reminds me of my good fortune. You see, 35 years ago when I developed cancer #1, colon cancer and had surgeries to remove my colon and give me a mucosal proctectomy, I needed to also walk at night. Being unable to take pain medication, walking helped a lot. Back then, as now, I am allergic to any pain killers or bowel medication. So, I walked and walked at night, but back then, my walking consisted of the living room and kitchen, two rooms about 12 X 12 feet. Not a lot of room to walk for hours or all night, but it was easier to catch myself when I felt faint from the dehydration. I could literally just reach out and hold onto the wall.

Today it is different. I have been through a few houses since then and about 12 years ago when we decided to knock down our then current house, and build a new one on the same spot, I had 3 requests. 1: I wanted a large kitchen, because I love to cook, 2: I wanted a main floor to be setup so I could walk continuously in a circle without having to turn and go back and forth. 3: Get rid of the walls; I need to see out. The windows keep me going, during my very long nights. I put the outside lights on and I can look into the woods and across the lawn all night (It makes my little world bigger). As with every plan, there is give and take. As it turns out, with a lot of windows, there are few spaces to put furniture against the wall, some windows are 12 ft. across.

The road I travel is filled with pleasing memories that help me stay focused, marching towards my goal. They help break up the thoughts of my condition. Walking through the kitchen warms my heart. It is the room where all social and all holiday events take place. Regularly I cook elaborate dinners for 30+- friends and family. They love to come for the food and the one man show of me preparing and cooking everything myself. I put up caution tape to keep everyone out of my working kitchen triangle. Everyone loves that I am a little nuts. If anyone must go to the pantry or refrigerator for something, they scamper by apologizing for the intrusion on my space.

Holiday meals are bigger, which may consist of cioppino, an Italian dish loaded with shrimp, lobster tails, clams, mussels, scallops, squid and topped with a filet of cod all in a zesty tomato sauce, homemade basil pesto over linguini, thinly sliced chicken breast lightly floured and fried to a golden brown covered in a succulent wine and caper sauce, broccoli rabe that has been lovingly sautéed in spices and olive oil, corn and balls of zucchini in a butter sauce. Don't forget the spirits, lots to go around. I have seven of those big, commercial, chrome roll-top buffets all set up; it is quite a picture. As my guests wait to eat, they also smell the home baked bread.

As I walk, I can smell the fragrances of the meals, hear the laughter, feel the warmth, the love that only food can bring together so tightly. It is more than just memories to me, it is visions of the food and the smiles etched in my mind and senses.

Walking through the kitchen, comforted by the memories, I know I must keep it together and continue these special and regular days for my family. It is my responsibility.

Walking this familiar journey is just part of my life, not necessarily a bad part, just a part. You see there really are only 2 outcomes. 1: I continue to walk and sip and get my hydration under control and maybe cause my intestines to open. Then during the following 3 to 5 days eat carefully,

4

only foods that I know will bring the enflamed bowel back into line, replace my electrolytes and get back into my life.

2: All hell breaks loose, the projectile vomiting continues and the blockages get worse, sending me to a local hospital, trying to get hydrated and my bowel moving, so I can drive 280 miles to my hospital in Burlington, Mass. and look at my options for more surgery. With all my complications, local hospitals are at a loss.

When I need to go to the clinic my wife calls my friend Dom and they put me in a car and in 3.5 hours I am in the hospital where they reconstructed all my insides. Don't know what I would do without my wife and Dom. I guess I've made their life more interesting and full of adventure.

I have had doctors through the years caution me about handling my condition myself, they warn me about a possible bowel rupture and major complications. I have a safety valve, so to speak for that, the vasovagal syncope, which is pretty amazing (not in a good way). When the pain mounts, the blood is shut off to the brain and I go down in a millisecond, I am out cold, no warning. One of the interesting things in dealing with it is you never know when you are going down. Stop walking and the blockage will get worse, so I cannot sit.

I try and keep walking and keep moving so I do not have a lot of pain. Good news is for the last 30 years, when I awake, things are a little better. My wife decided to get me a football helmet, but I prefer to walk on a path not close to furniture or sharp edges, and so far so good, I have always managed to crash to the floor and not hit anything. Of course, there are some nights when things don't go as well. When we lived in a small house in Madison, NJ, I blacked out while trying to vomit in the toilet and my head got stuck between the toilet and the base board heat. When I woke up with a red face, I had thought for a moment I'd been to the beach and had too much sun, but I could not remember any girls in bathing suits. During these bouts, I can easily lose 20 pounds in a few days. The balancing of the electrolytes and the weight gain takes about 3 weeks to get me back.

That is a brief over view of how I have lived from time to time over the last 35+ years, not bad if you consider the alternative of not living. As crazy as it sounds, I am in control. It's my life and 34 years ago I decided I was not going to lie down in the face of my illnesses, I was going to live and live life fully. Every day I try and do for others, build an equity base for my loved ones, work 10 to 12 hours (6 days a week), come home and spend time with my family and cook. Boy, I love to cook and I built the kitchen for it: 20+ feet long, 4 ovens, 2 Bosch dishwashers, lots of burners, 2 sinks (meat and a vegetable sink. I am very careful about bacteria), 2 butcher block islands in the middle of the kitchen, subzero ref, 30 feet of granite counter, seating for 14+ and 1,200 handmade 5 inch

X 7 inch floor tiles that are the end cuts of 400 year old reclaimed wood beams. I made every tile myself and hand rounded the corners and sanded them one by one.

I was lucky to find a very rich man who bought 40 foot reclaimed beams from the Chicago stock yards of yester year. He only needed 30 footers, so he cut off the ends and I bought them. I cut them to be perfect 5 inch X 7 inch beams and then laid them down and cut them ¾ of an inch thick, like you would slice bread. Then I sanded each one by hand and shaped the edges. I stacked them in my kitchen and sealed the room and put 2 dehumidifiers in the room and pulled the moisture out of the plywood floor and every tile stacked around the room. After about a week I started laying each tile in a bed of mastic glue. Soon it was time to grout. The grout was made of cork dust and glue. Unlike grout that you can push in and wipe off easily, this took forever to squeeze in the grout lines and finish off. Then I sealed the floor with a water base to keep the bright color of the wood. During this process, a few things happened.

First, let me tell you it took 4 weeks of work, 10 hour days on my knees. My knees were the size of footballs. I virtually could not stand up. My wife would walk in the room and say, with both hands folded together as she looked to the heavens. "Thank you God for making this his idea, not mine." It is beautiful and a floor I always wanted, my favorite room. Walking over it brings back memories of where I first saw it some 40+ years ago in a warehouse in Philadelphia. Walking over it makes me laugh, thinking of the task of making every one of the 1,200 tiles and installing them. Of course, there was also the thought of my lovely wife being so happy. She now had the best of both worlds, she could enjoy the beautiful floor, but never had to listen to me while I was doing it because it was all my idea.

So here I am in my mid 60's, having dealt with colon cancer (35 years ago) and the total removal of my colon and now dealing with a pouch made of my small intestines, hooked back up to my rectum. Find me in the shower and I look normal (though few who know me would use that word when describing me).

I have radiation and surgical scars on my neck from my last cancer, head and neck cancer 8 years ago. It has changed my ability to swallow and taste and destroyed my saliva glands. I deal with occasional head and neck infections from the radiation that ultimately attack my intestinal pouch and makes life even more interesting, but all and all, I'd rather be here than not.

With my hip, I developed avascular necrosis of the right femur head. Basically, the head of the leg bone died. By the time I found a study that met my search requirements, I was in 4th degree collapse and everyone else in the study was only in 2nd degree collapse. Long story short, the study failed and treatments all but disappeared. However, for me it worked, and I still walk on the same leg 30 years later. In 1984 I was given a maximum of 3 to 5 years before the hip would have to be replaced. Doctors wanted to replace the hip immediately. I can only guess they had operating room time they needed to fill.

I am not Mr. Universe, but I am clearly in better shape than most people my age and I work more hours than anyone I know. No question about it, I fall down from time to time, but I've put a plan together to get back to my life and that is what I do every day.

There is something else, I am a much better man fighting for my health than I ever was healthy. My diseases gave me a better understanding of foods, nutrition and exercise. It taught me how to read, I think I was reading at a 3rd grade level when my first cancer struck. Having to fight for good health, educated me, expanded my view of life and my world, humbled me and made me a man who both knows the value of becoming better every day and enjoys each day to the fullest.

Being up at night, dealing with my situations, allowed me to walk into my little girl's room and watch her grow. I would find myself taking a rest on the edge of her bed holding her hand while she slept, while blockages and dehydration were trying to take control of me and I would think to myself, *what a lucky man I am, to have this little girl depend on me.* I have to get back.

Those special moments when all things are muffled by the confusion that accompanies pain, exhaustion and dehydration and you are left with one overwhelming thought, it is then that you cannot help but realize the gift God has given you. Those few seconds holding her hand while she slept, before I continued my saunter, helped to keep me motivated.

Having said that, you would think she is my greatest gift in life. Well maybe so, but without my first gift, my wife, none of this would be possible. When I was going steady with her, I never took the time to see her value as a person. Lucky for me when I developed my first cancer, my wife (my girlfriend then) stayed right by my side; I owe it to her to make a good life for all of us.

For reasons I will never understand, she has stood by me, supported me and seems to love me. I have to tell you, I worry about her good judgment. She somehow feels that this is the deal and never falters under pressure. Always there, always strong and always with outstretched arms when needed, I got lucky – very lucky.

Together we have made millions, lost it and made it again. As crazy as it sounds, it is kind of what we do and during it all, we just keep coming back.

I have always been very public about my health. People in my social and business circles have seen me go from 175 pounds to 125 and back several times. They have seen me at work or home, very sickly looking. They have heard stories that I am dying on several occasions over the years, yet I reappear. I made no secret of my health problems. I learned early that you should tell everyone, because you may get some information that leads you to your salvation or a part thereof.

So, when friends encounter a health problem, it stands to reason that they would come see the guy who keeps coming back. I have had many people throughout my life come to my office or my home and ask me, how the hell do I keep coming back and how do I work so many hours? They follow with the question, how come you are still here? When asked, I always try and share what I know about picking a doctor, a health plan to go forward with, supplemental nutrition, exercise, meditation and diet, which are the keys to dealing with your situation. I also really want to transfer to them the importance of the gift of memories. I know I will never be able to make anyone understand how it relates to my life and how important it is to have a bank of wonderful memories of helping and sharing and doing for others, of building a life filled with battles, some funny and some sad, but I've won because I am still here. Fill your life with doing, yes doing, 24 hours a day without a break, making your life larger than was planned, a life that when it is over, or when you are fighting life and limb, you can reflect on the good memories. They may be all you have, so build a lot of them, they are your friends.

I have been taking creative writing classes. My teacher, Tom, has urged me to share what I have learned with others. One day he said to me, "What you know may save someone's life." So, thanks to Tom and his teachings, I've written this book. This book has one purpose in my mind, to give you options, to share with you what it took me years to learn. To let you know all things are not as they seem and there may be better choices. To give you hope in a hopeless situation.

CHAPTER 2
FROM THE CORNER

I did not realize it then, but at the age of about 7, I was being taught how to stay alive and conquer anything that came along. Lucky for me, because I would encounter a few bumps in the road ahead.

One cold night I sat in the corner of a cold cellar, bundled in a blanket. I was 7 and I did not know it then, but night after night I had the privilege of watching a man demonstrating the virtues of a hero. That observation would stick with me forever and one day, not only save my life, but give me the tools and heart to build a great life for my family, in spite of the obstacles ahead of me.

The man I was watching was my father. It was 1955 and reality for my dad was limited to a single vision, keeping my sister and me safe and together with him, as he held our shattered family together. My mom had died 3 years earlier from cancer and Dad was fighting medical bills and the task of properly raising 2 kids, along with running his laundromat and shoe repair. Yes, among other things, Dad was the little Italian shoe maker in the town of Springfield, NJ.

He was the best at what he did, he even made shoes. He fixed all his own Bendix washing machines and everyone knew he was the man who could fix anything. I loved Dad's store, it was called Courtesy Laundromat, which is exactly what it was. Dad loved his work, his customers and the privilege of having a business to build from. All the customers knew him on a first name basis and they all came in and yelled, "Hey Red, (Dad's nick name, because he had bright red hair) how are you today?" What a great place to hang out, for a kid. When Dad's business picked up, he hired a great shoe maker who was right off the boat from Italy. Adolph could not speak a word of English and it never mattered to him what the customer came in for, it was always 85 cents. You want heels, 85 cents, soles 85 cents, here to pick up your laundry, washed dried and folded, 85 cents. My dad tried not to leave him alone too often.

I watched my dad work hard every day, not for 8 hours, but 12 or 15, and sometimes what seemed like all night. He never complained, it was clear that he was on a mission. I thought it was the work that he loved so much, but later I realized it was the opportunity before him, he was grateful to have the privilege to work.

Watching him work long hours without any regrets and with a sense of pride, helped me. Later in my life, a disease was just something to beat, to work on and take control of, not a tragedy, but a task to overcome.

So here I am, 7 and wrapped in a blanket watching my dad work night after night. Back then the mob owned all the coin operated juke boxes, cigarette machines and washers and dryers. They did not like that my dad had started putting coin operated washers and dryers in apartment house basements, so one night they came in and filled the tub with cement, let some water in, let the machine start and then pulled the plug after the cement had gone through the entire machine, pump, hoses and all.

They should not have done that. They thought they would put some little helpless man out of business and teach him a lesson. Well, Dad was about 155 pounds, but he had no quit in him.

First on the agenda was to get the machines working. Dad had no money to buy new machines and if they were not working, the owner of the apartment house wanted them out of the building.

Night after night, I sat in that corner of that basement wrapped in a blanket as my dad took every inch of those machines apart and with a small chisel and hammer gently chipped every piece of cement out of the washing tub, the hoses and the pumps. It was not just one apartment cellar they hit, there were a few.

That blanket was an old quilt and the threads that crisscrossed would come out and my fingers would get tangled in them. Today, whenever a thread in my clothes or a blanket rubs along the inside of my fingers, I can smell the dampness of the basement and remember those special nights and the warmth I felt from this special man in a cold, damp, dimly lit cellar.

I had the privilege of watching him work throughout the night; I would fall asleep and wake up in the same place with him still working. He would work all day at the store, tend to both of us, feed us and then go to work all night freeing the machines of cement. Sometimes I helped, but I am sure I was more of a bother. From time to time he would look at me sitting in the corner and sometimes I would see a tear in his eyes. I heard sighs and gasps from time to time. Sometimes I was scared when I saw a tear in his eye, but the tear quickly disappeared and was replaced with a smile. Sometimes there was hurt and pain on his face, but there was always the humor and smiles to reassure me all was ok.

One by one the machines came to life. It was almost spiritual when the little red glow light went on and the water started to enter the machine. I sat there with a smile on my face as he ran the machine through its cycles.

There was more going on in that basement than a machine coming to life. There was a victory on so many levels, even spiritual. Dad's face told it all. I think he knew he was making another statement, one for the future of my sister and I, as well as himself. His determination and spirit said loud and clear, *this is my time and I will live it my way and no one will take from my family what is ours.* He is my hero.

I felt the spirit of achievement, the spirit of reward for not relenting and the spirit of family that bonded my dad and I with the moment. Clearly, I felt through all my father's elation that we were not alone. It was later in life that I came to understand that there are other entities, other forces just waiting to be a part of all of our lives.

He was not an athlete who threw a football one night and became a hero, this was a man who 24/7 was fighting to keep us together and provide for us. Back then it was very rare for a father to keep young children if the mother died. Usually they were raised by others within the family. Later in life, actually at his 90th party, he said, "You need to know, I was not holding you guys together, you were holding me, it was tough to lose your mom."

Having the privilege of seeing a person so devoted and so driven without pause, brought me into another reality of awareness that I have strived for and seldom seen in others.

The fact is I am on my second life threatening cancer and a devastating bone disease. I have been battling these diseases for 35 years+ and I know if it was not for the time I spent in the corner of that cold basement wrapped in a blanket, watching that no quit man, I would be dead by now. Instead, that experience and many others like it, opened my eyes to the fact that everything just may be in our hands.

Fortunately, he taught me at an early age to be silent and watch, you might learn something. Many times when I was very young and we would be walking in a poor section of a city, we would come upon a man sleeping in the street. My father would stop and say to me, "See that man, if he ever wants to tell you something, be silent and listen, he just might know something you do not know". Dad respected everyone. So, throughout my life, I watched and learned from the world around me and loved every experience.

As for those of you who are wondering why the mob did not come back, well, my dad is 99 and very much alive. Dad would not like the world to know all of his sides, so out of respect for my father, I cannot tell you how he handled those things. Let's just say he met with them and they never came back again.

Aside from being blessed with the privilege of watching a man with perseverance and focus strive to overcome insurmountable odds in that cellar, for me, was the birth of what happens when a person pushes beyond his or her limits and never relents. Something else is born and surrounds them with goodness. You can feel it, it is all around you and drives you to do better and greater things in life.

Despite my illness, my setbacks, I always try to help others. It gives me a sense of purpose and makes me a better man, a man much like my dad.

CHAPTER 3
RESPECT

Because there was no mom home, we ate out almost every night. My dad would fix the stoves, exhaust blowers and just about everything in the small coach diners where we ate for free sometimes. My favorite place to eat was Johnny Mulligan's Diner. It was a great place to eat with great people. These little diners had wheels on them, as they were made in a factory and towed to the site where they would rest. They built the cellar around them and if you were lucky enough to go into the cellar, you could still see the axels in the basement. There was one diner, called Gibson's, that only served breakfast and lunch and they had the axel hanging in the basement. That was my favorite for lunch. When I got older, I worked across the street and I ate my lunch there almost every day.

On some nights, my sister (Irene) and I sat in the booth alone while Dad was repairing something in the diner. He was only a few feet away and everyone in the diner watched us and talked with us, out of respect for my dad. Every night the same people came in to eat; it was a family.

The customers would put money in the juke box and let Irene and I pick the songs. I used to play 'Mr. Sandman' whenever I could. The diner was a real cast of characters. There was a man from Sweden who spoke little English and would literally drink 10 to 12, 8 oz. serving size cartons of milk. He would stack them up in front of him on the counter in a pyramid. We would bet on how many he would drink every time he came in. There was an old man who lived by himself and walked with a heavy limp and a cane. He always had a smile for everyone and a joke to go along with it. I think every knock knock joke in the world I heard first came from him. One of my favorite men was a tall black man who was a good friend of my dad's. His name was Slim. One day Slim sat with us and said, "Do you like horses? Would you like to come up to the farm and see a real race horse?" My sister and I were ecstatic. Soon after that on a Sunday, we went to the farm where Slim was a trainer and I rode a real race horse. It was the biggest animal I had ever seen. Today I cherish that my father never judged anyone by their color, religion or race. Dad opened his hands to everyone and gave them the opportunity to be a man or not. I had the good fortune to go through some 65 years of my life, without any prejudices, what a great gift he gave me. I watched friends have their lives negatively impacted by predetermined notions that have no validity, only to steal the good that life has to offer. It was a wonderful experience to see the respect my dad had for Slim and the respect Slim had for him; it brought the best out in both of them and those around them. It is a funny thing about respect, you can't buy it, will it or steal it, you must earn it, one deed at a time. People who do not even know you, can sense if you are a person who values others before you open your mouth.

At my favorite diner for dinner, (Johnny Muligan's) it was great fun to watch Johnny at the grill. He could pour pancakes with one hand and be flipping a steak with the other and all the time talking to me. To watch him when the diner was busy, was fun and he made it a game for me. It seemed like he was dancing. Running from the grill, to the stove, to the toaster, to the oven and putting plates together at breakneck speed.

Today, when we have many guests at our house I become these men I met through my dad, cooking many different dishes for 30 to 40 guests and bringing them to the table all at the same time. It is a well-choreographed dance, that plays out to a wonderful time for family and friends and I learned it standing next to my father, watching one man shows, in coach diners, as their owners prepared, cooked, plated, and served, all in one motion.

One night this one customer came into Johnny Mulligan's. I had seen him before and he was never nice to anyone. He never earned any respect, nor did he give any. On this night, my dad was fixing the oven in the back and I was helping. There was a pass-through window that the owner sent the finished dishes through and the server would take them and put them on the counter for the customer. The customer could see through the pass-through window, but could not see the grill, only the cook's head and shoulders. The man ordered a ham steak; I remember that because it was one of my favorites. Johnny put the steak on the griddle and then smiled at my dad, who was working on the oven close to the griddle. Soon the ham steak found its way to the floor and Johnny was standing on it, grinding it into the saw dust. Back then the cooking area of a restaurant was covered with saw dust and at the end of the night once the saw dust had caught all the grease and food, they would sweep it up and put down new saw dust. Johnny looked over to my dad," Hey Red, would you hand me that?" and pointed to the steak on the floor. My dad picked it up and handed it to Johnny. Johnny brushed it off and continued to cook it, all the time smiling through the window at the customer. Johnny served it to the guy and everyone watched him eat it, it was hard not to laugh. I never saw that man come back again. It is important in life to endear people to you and earn their respect. The respect you give is the respect you will receive. It will benefit you in many ways. My dad was a clear example of that.

I knew Dad was special because everyone respected him and was nice to him. When people needed things fixed, they went to my dad because they trusted him and knew they could depend on him. He had gained the kind of respect you earn inch by inch, deed by deed.

It was this respect that I saw the world had for my dad that helped me handle my health problems. The kind of respect you earn by your actions and deeds. It was this mindset that helped me earn the respect of my doctors and have them go the extra mile for me. Reading and learning about your health problem is so important, you must become informed. Question your doctor, but don't waste his time. Give him a reason to want to discuss options he may not discuss with another patient. A mutual respect will always benefit you in the long run.

Once I wrote a recovery outline for people who had suffered the same health situation as I did. My doctor read it and thanked me for it, but followed by saying, "Sam, the problem is that patients want help and not instructions, they come to us for answers, easy fixes as promised in all the ads. Seldom does a patient want to get involved 24 hours a day, 7 days a week. I appreciate this and there are some patients this will be beneficial for, but few."

If you are going to live to the fullest with your situation, you must get informed and research your options. The internet is helpful, unfortunately it is also filled with misinformation. Deciphering it is not really that difficult, just time consuming. I have found that if you keep reading test results and procedure results and outcomes of studies, soon the truth comes to the surface. Soon, you become informed and enlightened.

Never forget, it is very seldom that your doctor has been trained in nutrition and or understands it.

Also, doctors sometimes have tunnel vision, need to fill their operating card, or just think what they are doing is the best for you because of their limited exposure to other options. They are not bad people, just human.

When I had avascular necrosis, I sat with 8 orthopedic surgeons from some of the best hospitals in NJ and NY. 6 of them urged me to have my hip replaced immediately, for reasons that made sense to me at the time with the information I had at hand. I was in 4th degree collapse of the right femur head.

I started researching and after several months I found options. That was 33 years ago. What saved me was being informed and asking the right questions. I met with a doctor from a teaching university. After we talked and I questioned his suggestions (respectfully) he said to me, "Sam, come with me." We walked to his office and sat. "Sam, what is your back ground in the medical profession"? "I have none, I have just been sick a lot." He got up and closed the door and sat next to me. He said "You are right, a hip replacement has a life expectancy of 15 minutes to 7 years and if you are active, it will reduce it even more. The battery implants are as you said, a placebo. Remarkably they help with the pain, they do little more than that, the patient maintains their existing hip for a few years longer, which is a good thing. So, what else can I help you with?" I thanked him for his honesty and departed.

Because patients lack involvement in their own health, the doctor is forced to recommend the golden rule of medicine (what the drug companies recommend). When you get involved in your health, your diet and exercise, your doctor knows you are informed, involved and willing to work for a favorable resolution. It shows you have respect for yourself and your doctor will treat you differently and help you find better solutions.

It comes back to the same thing, you must earn respect to be treated like an equal. Your doctor must know that you are in charge of your health by being well informed, eating right, exercising and seeing your way through the hype of vitamin and mineral supplements. He must feel the need to work with you, because you are determined to improve your situation and not simply depend on him or her to somehow make you better. Believe me, there are a lot of great doctors eager to work with a patient who is really involved.

Your success is going to be a direct result of your efforts. This is a work in progress and only you can do it, no one can do this for you. By spending time systematically searching your options and learning to put a health plan together to aid your doctor's efforts, something else will be taking place. You will be gaining respect for yourself and start feeling better about your situation, because you are taking ownership and ownership is control. Take a page from my dad's life. Work every minute to improve your life, gain knowledge and fight for your place by earning the respect of others and yourself. Your doctors will respond differently to you. They will think twice about the drugs they prescribe, knowing that you are aware, and that can be the difference you need.

I cannot emphasize enough how important it is to earn the respect of your doctor. If you are working and fighting to improve your situation, respect grows on all fronts of every relationship and good things happen. When my dad defended his business against the men that were pouring cement into his machines, he made a statement. He said to a crime organization, "This is mine and I will fight to the end for it." It is a fact, that had they sent more men and more men, my dad would have lost, but to this day I believe they left his machines and him alone because they learned to respect him. You have to earn it. Earn the respect of your doctors and it will make a world of difference regarding whatever situation you might be battling.

CHAPTER 4
FRIENDS, TIME & FOOD

My first encounter with a doctor was when I was 3 years old. I know what you're thinking, how could I remember anything from the age of 3? Well, that was just prior to the year that the person who was closest to me and took care of me 24 hours a day, died. My mom had colon cancer and was misdiagnosed, mistreated and died when I was 4. Surprisingly the first 4 years of my life are stamped in my mind as if yesterday. Thoughts of those first few years of my life with my mom still comfort me during many long nights when sleep escapes me.

I remember the day my mom and dad were running their fingers through little round things on the porcelain covered metal kitchen table. It made a lot of noise and they were laughing and happy. I learned later that was the first bag of coins Dad had brought home from the coin operated washers and dryers he had put in an apartment basement, the start of a new business. Dad told me that they were saying to one another, they were going to be rich. There are so many wonderful memories of those first 4 years of my life that are like friends to me and comfort me.

At the age of about 3 my older cousins, Alfred and Anthony, thought it would be fun to each take a leg and an arm and swing me back and forth and then fly me across the room. Well, I flew beautifully, (actually I had little choice about the flight or the trajectory) like a graceful bird across the bed. All went perfect during the well-planned flight across the room, but there was that moment when my head stopped the flight as I smashed into the corner of the wall. I ended up with a big gash in my head that needed stitches. I don't remember much about the doctor, except he gave me a yellow plastic tool kit. It contained a hammer, pliers and a screwdriver. My mom liked him and they smiled at one another and he gave me toys, what's not to like. Early on I learned to like doctors, but of course that was the last time any doctor ever gave me tools.

At a young age, I felt that doctors were part of life and a good part. Through much of my childhood I had migraine headaches and at the age of 13 they were getting out of control. My father tried his best to find help for my headaches, but there was little help available. He took me to a doctor in Chatham, NJ. He shaved little spots on my head and stuck electrodes and performed some tests. It was not cool at 13 to have little bald spots, some things you just don't forget. I saw him a few times to no avail. I was a kid and had no idea what to do about my headaches, except to suffer. I had seen other doctors, but this doctor was a specialist. He gave me some medication that did nothing. Sometimes the headaches would get so bad I would pass out. Clearly, he had no idea what to do, nor did he understand vasovagal syncope, the reason why

I passed out. I was lost when it came to helping myself. However, I knew from listening to him, he was also lost. I am sure he was a well-intentioned doctor, but not capable of helping me.

My high school years were pretty much a blur. I enjoyed them to an extent. My headaches made it difficult at times, but the years passed. I lived next to an auto body and mechanical shop. And from time to time I would work on teachers' cars. I started hanging out in the shop at a very early age. At first I only cleaned up, then one day I started working in the body shop. I already knew how to fix dents, remove and treat rust and paint.

My dad would bring home the old coin operated washing machines and I would dismantle the machine from top to bottom and sand and paint everything and put it back together. When I got finished, they looked like new. My dad would put them back in apartment houses and the owners thought they were new.

Continuing to suffer from headaches I looked for answers. One day when I was about 14, I walked into a vitamin shop in Summit, NJ. The entire store was probably no bigger than 250 square feet. I walked in the store and was greeted by an old lady smiling from ear to ear. We talked and became friends. She was throwing a spice blender in the garbage and I asked her if I could have it.

"Sure, if you would like, I have another one also." As it turned out she had a few blenders, grinders and juicers that were not working.

"If you like, I can probably fix some of those for you," I said. I told her that I had been working with my dad since I was a kid and he taught me how to fix everything.

Our relationship had begun. From time to time, I would ride my bike up to her store and stop off and pick up juicers, blenders and grinders and fix the ones I could and return them to her. In return, she gave me vitamins and a beginning education about nutrition. Every time I stopped in she would teach me a little about spices, herbs, vitamins and minerals. This was back in the early 60s and taking supplements was not very common.

One day, she gave me a small book on sugar and the evil it possessed (I think those words were in it). Hell, I was a kid and I loved sugar and everything with sugar in it. It took me a long time to open that book and read it. I think that was a good thing because at the time she gave it to me, I would not have been receptive to it. It required cutting sugar out of my diet to control my headaches. This little book, a few pages, no larger than a pamphlet, was the answer to what countless doctors had missed. In all the visits to doctors to control my headaches, never once did a doctor suggest diet or

31

supplements as a possible way to control or mitigate my migraine headaches?

I eliminated foods containing sugar and foods that rapidly turned into sugar in my stomach and my headaches diminished significantly. I have to be truthful here, I cheated a lot. I paid for it when I cheated, but I still loved sweets. But I learned something here; I could control my health by what I ate. It was a pretty big revelation at the age of 15 to learn that all the answers for good health may not be in the doctor's office, there needs to be personal responsibility.

There was no mom in the house, so dad was the cook. When I turned 8, his lack of skill in the kitchen, motivated me to start cooking. I learned a lot from a great lady, my Aunt Helen. By the age of 15 I was very comfortable in the kitchen cooking many different styles of food and I loved it.

Early on I cooked simple meals. My first recollection of cooking for the family was lamb chops in the bottom of our stove which was the broiler. I baked chickens and broiled fish, some we caught and some we bought. Broiling and baking plain fish and meats, never frying any food. Salads with olive oil from Italy that my grandmother insisted I use, these were my meals. At that time, I had no idea that iceberg lettuce had about as much nutritional value as wet cardboard, early on I used iceberg, but sometimes I could find chicory at Jimmy and Less's grocery store on Morris Ave. and all three of us loved chicory. We ate salads every night filled with carrots and veggies and scallions.

My friend in the health food store gave me a bamboo steamer and I steamed my vegetables and sometimes fish. She gave me whole grain rice and flour and I started making breads. Pastas were a staple in my family and my Aunt Helen taught me how to make great tomato sauce, meat balls and braciole. I never fried anything and seldom cooked in cooking oil. It was simple basic food. Nothing from a jar, can, package or processed.

I did not know it, but I was cooking a basic Mediterranean diet. Throw in some beans, nuts and some fruit and bingo, there you have it. Funny thing about good food, it is simple. And the health benefits are numerous.

Here I was, no cook book, no training from a parent, but my basic instinct was to cook simply and healthy. I have thought about this from time to time and I have concluded that unfortunately we have been bombarded with ads to buy fast food, junk food, unhealthy food, and because our lives are so busy, we do it. Fast food, junk food, have become the quick meals to go to, but they are doing more harm than good.

When I was about 9, I was taught a valuable lesson. The lesson was that advertising is a lie. I was sitting in my house in Springfield on a Saturday morning watching cartoons.

There was a new product offered on TV. It was a well-known company that sold cereal in small boxes. They had come out with serving size boxes. I had never seen them before, but what grabbed me was they had several of them in a cardboard tray covered with cellophane. The person showing the cereal took the cellophane off and rolled it around in their hands and it disappeared. I jumped off the couch and ran across the street to Jimmy's grocery store and found the cereal in boxes covered in cellophane. I ran back home as fast as I could with the cereal under my arm like a football player running for the touchdown. I ran in the back door of my house and took the cellophane off and started rolling it around in my hands. I tried everything for probably an hour and yet the cellophane would not disappear. For me, that was the end of believing anything on TV, unless I could prove it to myself with facts. I have found George Carlin may have been right, everything is BS. The ads we see on the benefits of processed foods are all in the same category, false.

Just to be honest here, for many years, while I was building my businesses, I ate junk food often, but when I got home after 9 or 10 every night, I cooked a great meal of healthy food. Of course, once my health problems started, I immediately went back to my childhood cooking methods, of whole, real foods.

Never forget, most of what you buy in a bag, bottle, can or jar is dead. There are no enzymes in it, there are few vitamins of little value and it is not good for you. The life has been cooked and processed out of it.

I think it is important to understand that cooking takes time. I recommend that you take the time and learn to cook. Become proficient in the kitchen. I watch most people in the kitchen and what should take minutes, is a project for them. If you learn how to be proficient in the kitchen and really rock and roll, you will always have time to make good food. If cooking is not something you do well, you will submit to eating junk, which is something you definitely should not be doing.

Where to start. First, you must have a few good knives. I have several, but to tell you the truth Ron Popeil has a kitchen set that is hard to beat. I have knives that cost over $100.00 each and I use Ron's much more frequently. Then, pick a salad and its ingredients. Now, time yourself and give yourself 5 minutes to wash, cut and assemble the salad. Pick out a meal and time yourself for the prep and for the cooking.

Here is a healthy meal to start with. Walk into the kitchen and fill the pot with water and put it on high, cut up 6 large tomatoes and put them in a deep frying pan with 1/3 cup dry white wine (chardonnay) or vodka, ¼ cup olive oil, 2 teaspoons basil (dry), 2 chicken bouillon cubes, 4 cloves of chopped garlic, dash of crushed red pepper and turn on the heat high. Cut your salad up (5 minutes only). Add Mrs. Dash and olive oil and apple cider vinegar or lemon juice (red

35

vinegar will damage your stomach lining.) Your tomatoes have been cooking for about 10 minutes. Drop in your pasta and in minutes, you have fresh tomato sauce over a bed of linguini and a great salad. Cut up some whole-wheat Italian bread (unless bread disagrees with you) and you have a 15-minute meal that is delicious and healthy. I cook salmon, flounder, chicken cutlets, meats in all the same time. It is imperative that you are able to rock and roll in the kitchen or it will be a problem for you and you will resort to unhealthy foods. When preparing clams in red sauce, buy 24 little neck clams, put a pot of water on, wash the clams, bless them, then in a deep fry pan, I add dry white wine, basil, Italian seasoning, red pepper, lots of cut up garlic, 4 ounces of tomato paste, cover and cook it for 5 minutes, stir occasionally, then drop in the clams. Put the pasta in the pot (best with capellini) of boiling water, threw some Italian bread in the oven to warm (cut it open and sprinkle with garlic granules and olive oil if you like), cook the pasta until it is almost finished and then uncover the clams and remove them and set aside (now all open). Reach in the boiling water with tongs, take out the pasta and mix it in with the red clam sauce to finish and absorb the sauce. In 17 minutes you have another healthy, delicious meal.

Being able to produce a tasty, nutritious meal in a timely fashion is very important. I regularly rope off my cooking area in my kitchen with yellow caution tape when I am cooking for 20 or 30+. They get a kick out of it and alone I get the job done.

About the same time I was learning about health foods, I had a lesson about wasting life and it helped guide me through mine. I came downstairs on a Saturday morning, the first day of summer vacation. School was over and I was free. I sat in the living room eating a bowl of Cheerios for breakfast with my feet up on the coffee table. Dad walked in and said, "So, what are you going to do this summer?" "Well, Dad, Eddy and Jack said I can go to the town pool with them any time I like. So, I am going to hang out with the guys." Dad looked at me for a moment and calmly said, "Huh, finish breakfast and meet me in the back yard." You did not have to be a genius to figure out that this was not going to end well. I tried to drag out my breakfast as long as I could, but finally, reluctantly, I walked outside and Dad saw me coming and grabbed a shovel. "Come here, Chop." (Dad called me that sometimes.) I knew this was going to suck. He pointed to the ground and said, "I want you to dig a hole 6 foot deep, 6 foot long and 6 foot wide and then when you are done, dig another hole right here and put the dirt from the first hole in the second hole, and you keep moving that dirt around the yard until you figure out where you are working this summer." He handed me the shovel and went to work. I ran and jumped over the fence in the backyard and then I ran through the woods, about 2 miles, without stopping until I reached Springfield Garage (the garage that was next to my first house) and asked Mr. Briggs for a job. I started work the next day.

Dad hated wasted time. I think having lost Mom taught him that every moment was important. Dad was the least prejudice man I knew, however, he did not like anyone who wasted the gift of life. Dad always made it clear that a man or woman should be productive.

Throughout life, it has become very, very, clear to me that the gifts of success and the riches of life are always gained by effort. Man is the only animal in life that expects life to simply continue regardless of putting any effort into it or not. Every other animal works every day to survive or it will die.

People today become disillusioned too quickly. We are not dedicated to continuous effort, regardless of the result. We waver and change direction, looking for the next quick fix. Luck, as it is called, is made, earned, not found. If you are lucky with maintaining your health or avoiding any serious money problems, you earned it. More importantly, you are likely to enjoy what you earned, because you put in the effort to get there.

Unfortunately, one program after another seems to instill complacency into our hearts. I noticed something about myself through my illnesses. When I am healthy enough to work and produce, I am a different person. I understand the release of endorphins and the high you get from them, but it is more than that. I can see and feel the long-term benefits of hard work and perseverance.

Conversely, when I have been sick and I am recovering, not able to function, not thinking clearly and unable to produce, I feel vastly different about going forward. It is then that I must trust a plan to go forward that I am accustomed to and wait for a mental and physical clearing.

As individuals, we work hard to buy the things we want. So too in life, we need to work hard to maintain good health. Laziness and complacency will prevent you from that goal. You need a plan to recover your health and then tend to it 24/7. Recovering from an illness or living well with one takes effort. You need to eliminate all sugar, maybe flour and all processed foods. Eat whole foods and don't be afraid of lean meats (but limit them) and eggs. Eat vegetables and never eat store bought dressing for your salad (apple cider vinegar or lemon juice with real olive oil). Stop eating processed foods. They are poison to your body, both physically and mentally.

Exercise. Yes, you must exercise. If you do not exercise, everything is lost, I think exercising is #1 and here is why. If you eat well, and exercise, it makes you feel good about yourself and you have a greater desire to eat better things.

We have been conditioned to take it easy and let the system help us, be it doctors, government or our religious leaders. In a nut shell, your best support is yourself. Many years ago, I started making a simple daily plan for recovery from my financial problems and health problems. During the battle with my cancers, I literally lost millions and had to rebuild my fortune or live a simpler life. I put the diet plan on paper and condensed it to a business card size. My business card would remind me to eat the following every day: Breakfast, 2 eggs, put ¾ cup of strawberries, ¾ cup of blue berries, cod liver oil, a few vitamins like C, D, protein powder, acidophilus, into a blender and drink it for breakfast. I did this every day, no matter how it tasted. For my dinner, it was beets, cabbage and carrots in the juicer, I drank it. And I did it every day as my card instructed. For me, it is always about the piece of paper. I am lost without it, my emotions will sabotage my plan every time. When I follow a schedule to recover and I stick with it, it works.

Find or create a set of 20 to 30 nutritious, healthy meals you can prepare easily and rotate them. If you are in the process of recovering and may not have your normal energy, lay out the cook time and ingredients so it is easy for you to prepare.

We must be proactive to the pitfalls waiting for us tomorrow. Set a plan, reduce it to a business card and stick with it. Remember, life is always about what you do first.

CHAPTER 5
RESPONSIBILITY

When I was about 17 years old, I was out on a date with a young lady and eager to put an end to the date. It was one of those nights I needed to be alone. It was a full moon and I was better alone. I pretended to be sick and politely took her home.

On this night, the air was cold and crisp, a perfect winter night with temperatures below freezing. The sky was clear and I wanted to be in a place where I could feel whole.

Tonight, I would treat myself to be touched by my maker. No, I am not a man that enters the doors of my religious gathering hall regularly, but I get it. I know who I am beholding to and what treasures can be had just for letting my maker in.

When I reached home about midnight, I made some sandwiches, dressed in my warm hunting boots and gloves and put my dog, Duchess, in the car. Off we went and Duchess was ecstatic. She knew exactly where we were going. She sat up on the front seat looking over the dash board as we drove about 60 miles to the Delaware Water Gap, in my 1967 Pontiac Tempest Lemans, with a small block 326 v8, 4 speed on the floor, black bucket seats and a convertible top. We listened to my favorite tunes. Johnny Mathis was singing all my favorite songs being played from my 8-track player I had installed on the floor. The 8-track player was a model Belair BP 323, funny that I found the receipt just last week some 45 years later. Oh, and I still have the tape player and tapes; wish I still had the car. Duchess was a Hungarian Vizsla. She was on the large size for this breed, about 70 pounds. Duchess was a very expensive show dog and not something we would buy. A very rich lady could not control her, so she gave her to my dad.

My dad trained her to be a pointer for hunting small game. Duchess was something to see on the open grass fields, tracking and pointing her quarry. Everyone wanted to buy her from my father whenever we hunted. To my dad (lucky for me) this animal was family.

So, with my best friend sitting on the front seat next to me, we headed off. As we got closer to the Water Gap, it started to snow, and there was already about 6 inches on the ground from an earlier storm. We arrived at the Delaware Water Gap and got off the highway and took a road that took us to the edge of the river and the foot of the mountain. I had a few favorite spots where I would park for my walk up the mountain. We parked the car and set out on foot. It was snowing, and although the sky was cloud covered, you could see well, as the full moon's light pushed its way through the night sky and snow-filled clouds.

Off we went, to walk to Sun Fish Pond on the top of the mountain. There is a great trail on the other side of the mountain that is part of the Appalachian Trail, but it is a lot longer as it is a gentle trail; the trail we took was steep in places and shorter. The trip up was as expected with a snow-covered mountain, a little slipping and sliding, but a controllable climb. We both had made this trip many times in the night and knew the area. Actually, I never started up the mountain in the daylight, so all of my references were at night, shadows of the surrounding valleys and mountains. When you enter the woods at night it takes about 45 minutes for your eyes to fully adjust.

As we got higher in elevation, the snow changed to rain for about 1 hour and back to snow again. Now with about 8 inches of snow on the ground, I was concerned with the layer of rain. If the rain freezes and then is topped with snow, it will be difficult walking back. When you step, you will be temporarily supported by the frozen layer of rain and then fall through and crush the snow below. It makes for a very tiresome walk.

Soon we reached the pond in all its glory. Long stretches of the frozen lake were surrounded by rocks and trees touching the water's edge with their branches pulled to the earth and frozen lake by the weight of the glistening snow. The moonlight was almost undetectable by now as Duchess and I sat on the edge of the lake enjoying the serenity. As I did, I

43

realized, how much I truly love the gift of the woods at night and the ability to blend in rather than disturb the grace of the night. Then I laughed a little, thinking of how I fell in love with the night years ago and learned to be still and let it surround me.

As we walked along the edge of the pond, I noticed that someone had propped up a few branches against a tree as somewhat of a shelter. We walked over to it and pushed our way in. I cleared the snow and we sat. We sat in the perfect spot looking down a long stretch of the lake. Duchess climbed up on my legs and we shared a sandwich, both of us quietly looking at the pond, the falling snow, the dim light of the night and the occasional clump of snow falling from an overloaded branch. Across the pond, the world seemed to shimmer with life that can only be seen in such moments. The forest was quiet, as even the nocturnal hunters had bed down for the storm. Finally, I was with me, the me that is larger than who I am as an individual. I could see who I wanted to be, who I was supposed to be without distraction of man or man's creations. This is as close to my heaven as I am able to get. No clergyman was speaking his profound words, in hopes I would hear the word of God, but yet the Creator's work was coaxing me to take stock of the gifts before me, assuring me that life is a gift and one who allows the gifts to be a part of them, will find their way. I always came home a better person.

I was well dressed for the night, but a warm drink always made it better. I had a thermos filled with hot chocolate in the game pouch of my hunting jacket. As I poured a cup, I remembered something that is an inescapable recall every time I pour from a thermos. It was some time ago when a man told me a story. He said, "There were three men who arrived at the pearly gates. Saint Peter said to them, "Welcome my children, welcome to heaven. Before you enter the Kingdom of God, please tell me the greatest thing you have ever seen or heard." The first man said it would have to be the parting of the Red Sea. Saint Peter said, "Enter my son." The second man said, "For me, Father, it would have to be giving of one's life to serve others as in the clergy and so many other selfless people around the world devoting their life to serve the less fortunate." "Some of my finest work my son, enter." The third man said, "Well, I guess for me it would be the thermos bottle." "The thermos bottle, my son?" The man stood his ground and said, "Yes, my Father, the thermos bottle." "What is so great about the thermos bottle?" Saint Peter asked. "Well Father, you see, you put in hot stuff and it keeps it hot all day long. You put in cold stuff, and it keeps it cold all day long, HOW DOES IT KNOW?" (Some things never leave you.)

For a while it became one of those once in a lifetime nights. Silent snow, moon lit clouds with moments of darkness, clear views of a scenic pond and a good friend. We must have drifted off, but soon the howling wind and blinding snow awoke me, serenity was over. The snow was so heavy I was not sure where the pond now lay. I knew we had to get moving. Duchess was still on my legs and she looked at me as if to say, now what?

I got my bearings and we started down the mountain. The side we came up has a trail, but I knew the mountain and the trail was a distance from me, so I took off, cutting the trail short as I did so many nights before. As I expected and earlier feared, the snow was about 4 inches with a layer of ice and then more snow. It was slow going. The snow was so heavy that it was difficult to keep my direction. I knew I was off my normal course and probably not going to come out on Old Mine Road where I had entered the woods, but it did not matter. I knew the valley, the mountain range in the night, and when I got close to the road, I would know exactly where I was.

The going got tougher as many of the areas were small rock drops and you had to walk along the mountain to avoid them, rather than go down. That night it seemed there were more small impassable cliffs than ever before. It seemed we were going back and forth rather than down. The blinding snow in the forest was challenging. Duchess was not her usual self, she was not running in front scouting, she stayed inches from me. Soon I realized her feet or legs were cut. The ice between the snow layers or shale were seriously hindering her. We stopped and I tried to help, but there was nothing I could do. I wanted to carry her, but now I was moving from tree to tree and the snow, wind and mountain had taken their toll on me. I reassured her by my gentle words, letting her know we were ok.

We pushed on. Fatigue set into my every joint, but soon we reached Old Mine Road, a place that I knew meant safety. Standing on this old road, I looked to the left and then to the right. Across the street was the river. All the landmarks of the mountain ranges and river valleys were gone, obscured by the driving snow. I could only see about 30 feet in the driving snow.

There was a small ditch alongside the road and we huddled there for a moment. I knew this road was seldom traveled in the winter and if I was going to get to my car, it would be of my will and wits. Back on the road I looked around. Every fiber in my body that was fueled by prior successful ventures in the area told me my car was to the left. We started walking. It was daylight now, but visibility was still limited. The going got harder. My feet were cold. My hands and torso were no longer comfortable. Luckily I knew not to work up a sweat or it could be the end. We walked, stopped, and walked and rested, and soon found myself sitting on the side of the road on a rock with my friend on my lap. With her head buried in my coat between the buttons, I held her close trying to protect her from the elements.

It was then that I realized, this living, trusting creature was my responsibility and I was letting her down. My father taught me all my life, by his words and deeds, that you protected family and friends and others who cannot protect themselves.

I decided to continue in the direction I was traveling. Within an hour I was worn out, I sat again. The day was getting short and the snow had continued. I felt as though I had left my principals in another place far from my decision making process. I had put my loved one second to my urges. I knew it was about the night, the full moon, so many times before I had made bad decisions during a full moon. This was the worst. I had been so self absorbed in my inner emotions, not my calculations. I remember asking for forgiveness.

Weak and cold, I started rethinking my direction. Visibility was still poor and I decided to go the other way and abandon what my heart told me was the right direction. I had to try something new. We walked and walked in the other direction. It was dark, but the snow let up a little. I found myself sitting on the side of the road in a small ditch that ran along the road. There was little wind there, and there in my deepest thoughts, I knew I was in trouble. I don't remember how long I was there, but there I sat. It seemed all hope was lost. Maybe it was time for a fire. I smoked, so I had matches. Finding dry wood would be a problem. But what else could I do?

Just then Duchess, who was sitting on my lap with her head in my coat between the buttons, startled. I heard nothing at first. Then I could hear the slow crushing of snow by a car's tires. I sprang up just in time as an old pickup truck stopped. Those old Fords had simple 6 cylinder motors that ran quietly because of all the metal around them, gas mileage was a non-issue so they piled the weight on. I would have missed it, if not for Duchess. I hurried to the door with Duchess in my arms and a man pushed the door open. I blurted out, "Can my dog come in?" He said, "Son, your dog comes in first." He told me he saw my car back a way and wondered what it was doing there. Then he said, "I saw your footsteps going and coming and hoped I would run into you." He turned the pickup around and we went in the same direction I first walked. By now the snow had all but stopped. "There you are son, why don't you leave the dog here and get your car started." I was only 50 or 60 feet away from my car when I turned and doubted my intuition.

This was another lesson that night; never backdown from your goals, convictions and dreams. How well did I learn that? Well, at least to a fault. I had been about 60 feet from my car when I doubted my intuition and turned around in the snow. We have all heard it before in so many forms: "All things come to he who believeth." "Our doubts are traitors and often make us lose the good we might achieve by trying".

49

For the rest of my life, for better or worse, I have stayed on track till it hurts and then kept going with very little regret.

I fired up my car, warmed it up, and cleaned off the snow. While this was going on, the man held Duchess in his warm truck. I walked to the truck and opened the door and he asked, "Do you know how to get out of here, are you alright?" I had food and gas and told him I was ok. "Ok son, I will be back through here in about 4 hours and I will check to see if you are still here." I got Duchess and thanked him and he drove off. That man saved my life with a simple gesture. (You never know when something so small might be so important to another).

We sat in the Pontiac and warmed and drank and ate. I thought about what I had done. I violated everything I knew about being prepared. And more importantly, I risked a life I was responsible for. I made a mistake and no matter how hard I tried, I'd been unable to protect someone who was in my care and custody.

That night taught me to be aware of all around me and never put anyone at risk. From that day forward I looked at life differently and how I perceived my responsibility to others. Fact is, because of that night, I am indeed a better person, father, boss and friend. And it goes without saying I am richer, richer and closer in the search of mastering the 5 riches of life: social riches, spiritual riches, financial riches, health riches and emotional riches, my never-ending quest.

I have come to believe that all of life's greatest and worst moments are our responsibility. We make the choices. At some level there is a natural order not dictating but listening to our every decision. We really are more dynamic and have more control of our destiny than society teaches us.

We have a responsibility to our loved ones to be an asset to their lives. To do this, we need to be prepared and productive. To do this, we must make the right decisions. Not the ones that may feel good at the moment, but ones that will make us stronger and more knowledgeable.

Preparation for health and prosperity is not optional, it is how life is supposed to be. Eating healthy and exercising are a must. Let me be candid with you. I never liked exercising, it is job for me, but because of that, I feel a greater reward for making myself do it.

For those of you who have a lot of excess weight to lose, let me share something with you. Personally, I am not fond of those who say, "Why don't you just stop eating?" And to that, we now know that calories are handled differently by many. Exercising and dieting may not be the total answer. It seems if you diet and deprive yourself of food, your body has a defense mechanism that detects the lack of food and slows your resting metabolism dramatically. Meaning, that your body burns very few calories while you are at rest. It is a self-preservation mode taking place that is a holdover from many years ago when food was hard to find and meals were sometimes difficult to come by.

Eliminate sugar, flour and eat a high quality Mediterranean diet and exercise. It is paramount that you exercise. A simple set of dumbbells found in Walmart can get you started. If you have never exercised to build muscle, get help. When I am trying to gain muscle, I start cooking fish and lean meat and a lot of chicken. All these proteins are simple to cook and fast. Cod, salmon and flounder are 3 of my favorites. Cook with stainless or cast iron inside, the nonstick and aluminum insides, are not good for you.

Fish:

- ❖ 3 tablespoons of good olive oil
- ❖ 5 cloves of chopped garlic sautéed for 2 minutes
- ❖ 20 +- ounces of diced tomatoes, fresh or canned with juice
- ❖ Dash of crushed red pepper (if you can handle it)
- ❖ Tablespoon of dried crushed basil
- ❖ 2 small or one large chicken bouillon cube
- ❖ A dash of dried Italian seasoning
- ❖ ½ cup dry white wine (I use the cheapest white wine)

1. Cook on high, boil rapidly for 5 minutes to 10 minutes, add a little water if you need to, it should be wet like a loose sauce.

2. Cut your cod fillet into portions and place them into the sauce and cover it with the sauce.

3. Season with salt and cover, simmer low for about 5 to 10 minutes or until the fish is flaky white (make your 5-minute salad while it is cooking).

4. With a spatula, put the portioned cod in a shallow dish and with a spoon scoop some of the sauce on it.

5. Garnish with freshly chopped parsley and serve with a good Italian or French bread. Accompanied with your salad with olive oil and lemon dressing. Protein, fish oils, lycopene and selenium. Vitamins and minerals. And you did it in 15 to 20 minutes.

Chicken:

If you like chicken, it is almost the same, using a deep frying pan add:

- ❖ 3 tablespoons of good olive oil
- ❖ 5 cloves of chopped garlic sautéed for 2 minutes
- ❖ 20 +- ounces of diced tomatoes, fresh or canned with juice
- ❖ Dash of crushed red pepper (if you can handle it)
- ❖ Tablespoon of dried crushed basil
- ❖ 2 small or one large chicken bouillon cube (optional)

❖ A dash of dried Italian seasoning

❖ ½ cup dry white wine (I use the cheapest white wine)

1. Cook on high, boil rapidly for 5 minutes to 10 minutes, add a little water if you need to, it should be wet like a loose sauce.
2. While this is cooking, slice a chicken breast in half so you have 2 flat pieces.
3. In another frying pan put:
   2 (more if needed) tablespoons of good olive oil
4. Add 4 cloves of chopped and crushed garlic
5. Heat on medium high and brown chicken in olive oil and season with salt and pepper as cooking (do not overcook, just brown slightly).
6. Take chicken out and cut into 1-inch cubes and place them in cooking sauce. Cover and cook all together on medium low.
7. Slice Italian bread and lay it in the pan you cooked the chicken in, rub it around and heat and soak up all the oil and bits of heaven.
8. Lay the bread on the sides of a shallow bowl and scoop the chicken and sauce into the bowl and make sure the bottom of the bread is in the sauce, garnish with parsley. Serve this with your 5-minute salad.

One of my staples has always been real brown rice. This takes longer, but if you make a batch you can always freeze it in portions and just warm it later. My favorite way to cook brown rice is in a pressure cooker:

2 cups brown rice (washed) and 4 cups water (depending on the pressure cooker you may have to add a little more water, you will know when it is done for next time), 2 tablespoons butter, dash of salt, close the lid to your pressure cooker and cook for about 50 minutes to 60 minutes. Turn flame up high until the pot starts to blow steam out of the vent and then turn it down all the way (if your pot burns the first time, you may have to get a flame diffuser to put under the pot). If you hit the time just right, the butter and bottom of the rice will have caramelized and you will end up with a soft fluffy rice with a lightly caramelized bottom, that spreads a nutty flavor that enhances the entire pot of rice.

If you exercised today, cooked and ate one of those simple dinners, I guarantee you will feel better, namely because you're doing things to improve your health. Sorry no coffee or dessert, we are trying to send a message to every cell in our body, "I am now taking ownership, I AM COMING BACK".

Whenever I am re-establishing my health after a health crisis or rebuilding my fortune after I lost it due to my failing health, one thing is certain, I put an educated plan together, from solid statistics. Never turn from your goal. Make sure your plan is fact based not emotionally driven. A note, if you are not as healthy as you would like to be, gather information from reliable sources, talk to professionals, create a plan and then follow it through.

Once you have a plan, conviction is paramount. Follow that 24 hours a day, 7 days a week, until it is part of you, you need to feel this in your heart. Don't worry if you get derailed from your plan, just start immediately again. If you really want to succeed, your plan should be a daily routine. Exercise, eat healthy, keep a positive attitude, set a goal and stick to it. Write this down and post it somewhere you can see it every day. It's a reminder that you are on a journey to a better you.

CHAPTER 6
CLOCKED

As a young boy I worked at Springfield Garage. They sold GMC trucks and fixed everything that had tires. At about 18, I was pretty good at fixing and painting cars and trucks. The boss was Bob Briggs, a great guy. His 2 sons, George and Bruce, worked there and they all treated me like family, just a great first full-time job. Bob let me stay at night and the weekends and work as much as I liked. I was painting friends' cars and that made me pretty cool with the older guys. In the corner of the body shop there was an old cabinet of shelves and in it were old grinders, polishers and electric hand tools that had seen better days. I liked to fix motors and equipment, so I would take them apart and try and repair them and bring them back into service.

One day, on a high shelf in the cabinet, I found an old machine. I blew all the years of dust off it with the air hose and discovered it was a very old time clock. I showed it to Bob and he said I could have it. I had no idea at the moment, but finding this machine was part of the answer to so many things in my life. It was a pile of junk to say the least. There was no cover and all that was there were the insides. I took it home and from time to time I worked on it. There was no hurry to fix it. Actually, I thought I might use the inner workings to make something else one day. It had a trip hammer and I thought I might use it to make a boxing round bell, but I never did.

One day I finally cleaned it, greased it, and put it back together, and to my surprise it worked. It kept perfect time and sections of the ribbon had enough old ink to actually print the time dark enough to see. I put it in the cellar and went on with my life.

It was not long before I wanted more money. Springfield Garage was a big shop for the day with several mechanics, but there were only 3 body men and I was one of them. I had friends in the business and they told me about the new trend in the body business, piece work. Shops were paying their employees by the job and not by the hour. You would get so many hours at your pay rate to do a job and if you finished early, you made more money. I convinced Bob to put me on piece work.

In the early goings it was tough, as there were so many distractions it was hard to stay focused. It was everything from someone telling a joke, to helping a mechanic push a car in, to going to lunch. I fought from being distracted and soon it seemed to smooth out and I was making the same money I made from straight hourly pay. I started to notice the down time that took place during the day: coffee break, lunch, another coffee break, stopping to light a cigarette, talking to customers and on and on.

I knew if I was going to make money I had to work smarter.

One night I had an idea, I would bring in the time clock and start punching in and out every time I stopped for anything. If I lit a cigarette, I punched out, and when it was lit and I was working again, I punched in. When I went to the bathroom, I punched out and ran back to punch in and start working again. I was running everywhere, I became obsessed with the time clock. I kept it from everyone except Pete, my fellow body man. I knew everyone would think I was nuts. Soon I started to time my jobs. If the book was going to pay me for 2 hours to hang a fender on a car, I needed to do it in 1. The race was on.

I started tightening everything up and counting every minute of the day. For lunch I would go to Donny Gibson's coach diner, which was across the street. I knew Donny since I was 4 and I literally lived across the street. I said to Donny, "Would you do me a favor?" "Sure, what do you need?" There was a small window above Donny's grill and he could see Springfield Garage from the window. "When you are at the grill and see me running down the street at 12 o'clock, would you put up today's special." Donny laughed and said "Chip, you are in here about 15 minutes for lunch as it is, are you trying to cut it to 5?" "I know, I am just trying to beat the clock." And so it was from then on. At 12 noon I would come running out the front door of the shop and Donny would see me coming. Donny always had the special of the day on the counter for me. Boy, I loved his meat loaf and beef goulash. The mashed potatoes and green beans were to die for, plenty of gravy and 2 pieces of Donny's rye bread already buttered.

Donny seemed to get a kick out of my routine. This was real home cooking at its best. I allowed myself 5 minutes to get it down and pay Donny and off I would go with a piece of coconut custard pie in my hand running across the street. He had the best coconut custard.

I was back in the shop and working in less than 10 minutes. I cut out breaks; I pushed myself to keep my communications short with everyone. If you are thinking I was a little nuts, you are not alone. Everyone in the shop thought I was nuts, but I was on to something.

The fact is, we all cared about each other, and they were all great guys, but I was going someplace different and that did not sit well with some. I wanted to go to a bigger body shop to make more money. I drove to Maxon Pontiac in Union NJ (now Maxon Honda) and there I looked around and found the service writer, his name was Vince. I asked him for a job and he said, "We do not need help."

I said, "Let me have 2 spots (this way I could work on 2 cars at once) for 2 weeks and if I do not do more than double the work of anyone you have, you keep my pay."

He looked at me and said, "Ok kid, you are on, what do you do?"

"I am a combination man."

"Do you paint?"

"Yes, I paint, I do light frame work, front end work, plastic and any kind of heavy collision work on anything from small cars to heavy trucks."

He laughed and said, "Sure, don't they all, but what will you not do?"

"Mr. H, if you put a ton of shit over there and give me a spoon and tell me to move it, I will, I come to work and make money, not play."

My clock and I shocked everyone, and soon I was the shop foreman. They called me the "streaker" because I ran to lunch and ran to the bathroom and everyplace else I went. Bottom line, I was making a lot more than anyone else in the shop. It was not long before the owners got wind of me and I was given the choice jobs. Sometimes I had three cars apart. While the plastic was setting on one I was pulling another apart between applying coats of paint on another.

When the shop went on strike, I found a small garage for rent up the street. It was the back of a small gas station about a mile west on Rt. 22. It was no more than one big overhead door and enough room to put in one 18 wheel tractor. A friend knew the owner and took me to meet him.

The landlord, Joe, had a trucking company next to the gas station. I was a little nervous because I had heard that Joe was in the mob and I did not know what to expect. We came to terms and for the first month's rent, I agreed to fix the left corner of a black Mack tractor cab that was crushed in a jackknife accident. The job was worth about 3 times the month's rent, but I had my shop. I called it Courtesy Auto Body. I named it after my dad's Laundromat, Courtesy Laundry.

The gas station out front was the only diesel supplier for miles and work poured in from truckers. I worked 16 to 18 hours a day and alone, unless I had an overnight paint job, then I worked 24 hours. I tried to hire a few guys to help, but they hated that they were working for the 'clock,' as one said. So, day after day, night after night, I worked alone.

I started a paint program, where, if you brought me your truck by 5pm, I would pull it outside, regardless of the temperature or weather, and pressure wash it, pull it in, fix small dents, sand every inch and get it ready for paint. I set a schedule for the night, and my clock and I went to work. It seemed I always finished ahead of the times I set. My bottom goal was to have the truck masked, sanded, sealed and ready for paint by 2am. I'd shoot the rims and frame first with paint. Let them cure with the latest catalyst for 60 minutes and draped them with a frame to hold the canvas off the frame and paint the cab.

I would put heat lamps on the front doors to speed up the drying so my lettering guy could work safely at 7am.

By 8 am the next day, the truck was ready for pick up.

One day I was taking in a truck at about 5pm and Joe was getting gas for his new Cadillac. He asked, "What are you doing to that truck?" I said, "I was fixing the dents and painting it."

As always, I worked all night and about 7:30 in the morning, I pulled the truck out and was removing the last little bit of masking paper. My friend, Harry, pulled up and started lettering the door for the customer.

Joe pulled in with his Cadillac and came over and said, "Hey, Sammy, this isn't the truck you pulled in last night, is it?" I was very tired and without being disrespectful I said, "Yes, I've got some things to finish, I've got to wrap it up." I continued to work, as Joe walked away and got in his car.

This was 1971 and I was charging $500.00 per truck and doing them in one night, it was a lot of money. One day Joe came over and said, "Sammy, I want to talk with you, let's go and have coffee."

We sat at a table and made small talk. He had a great sense of humor and was really a great guy.

Joe said, "Sammy, can you do this to any truck in one night."

"You mean paint it?"

He nodded.

"No problem." I said

"Kid, we are going to make a lot of money." Joe smiled

A new chapter of my life began: I would get a truck from Joe shortly after the sun went down and it had to be ready to pull a load to Chicago or Mass. by sun up. I was introduced to a very handy guy named, Billy, from the south Jersey swamps. Billy would come in while I was fixing the dents and prepping the truck and make the serial numbers match the new bill-of-sale.

I got paid $1500 to $2000.00 per truck. There was no rhyme or reason why I got different prices, but who cared, in the early 1970s, that was a fortune.

You would think by now I had little use for the time clock, but it was my task master. It helped to keep me going during those long nights. More importantly, it kept me on track during the short nights in the summer.

As I went through life, that time clock always stayed with me. If not in physical form, certainly in my thoughts as I approached any project.

For me, the clock was the answer to my lack of education.

Life is about a goal with a time limit. Time is begging to be appreciated and used wisely, not wasted. We are here for a very short time. Set time limits for your recovery. Be realistic but demanding. Every plan must have a goal and a time in which it is reached. Improve your health, the same way. Start with the smallest of things. Cooking dinner, allow yourself so much time to finish. Get creative and it will easily become part of your life. Start using that clock for everything you do to recover and soon it will amaze you. Be determined to beat the clock, not watch it.

To this day, I still clock myself during a recovery. It is too easy to be emotionally involved with your health and feel depressed about it and do little. To really be fair to a recovery, and in order to see signs of improvement, you need a schedule and a clock. We have our doctors, friends and family urging us to take it easy, but we need to help ourselves. It is our problem, not anyone else's.

When I have been really beat up by an illness and starting a comeback from zero, I start with a bike I have, one with arms attached to the pedals. When I push the arms forward and back the pedals go around and likewise, if I peddle it, the arms go back and forth. I find that it is a low impact cardio with some muscle building. Of course, I clock my time and my speed, every day or every other day, increasing the time by a minute. Soon, I move to dumbbells. This is where I start feeling better, feeling as if I'm om a recovery to better health. I like to start early, first thing in the morning. I pedal the bike to get things moving a bit. I time myself to a set goal. Then I start with a set of curls with my dumbbells. I pick up a weight that will allow me to do about 10 reps before it gets strenuous. Then I go upstairs and cook 2 scrambled eggs. I allow myself 10 minutes to cook them and eat them and back to the weights. 10 reps again and back upstairs, watch that clock, don't let your emotions stop you from a recovery. Strawberries, blueberries, half a banana, acidophilus, a few vitamins and a teaspoon of turmeric (I buy organic turmeric at $10.00 a pound on ebay, great for inflammation during recovery), a little water and blend. Drink it down and back to the dumbbells. Another set with heavier dumbbells and back upstairs. I have found that during a recovery it is best to exercise one group of muscles at a time. If you worked on your legs and arms together, you will probably feel very tired that day and possibly for several days. Don't rush it. Tomorrow, if you are not exhausted, take on your chest with bench presses or pushups. Do not exercise your arms again until they feel strong and have fully recovered. For me, at this age, it takes 3 to 4 days before I can curl weights again.

When you have a plan for recovery and stick to it, something happens, you just earned your day. I love the fact that every day I have a manageable day where I feel good. It is a product of my discipline, my hard work and my plan. It is my day, I earned it. Other people just waste their days and go through them like they have an endless supply, but I earned my day and my day is mine, it is a good feeling to have earned a day and not wasted it. It fills your soul with pride, a humble pride, because only you know your story. It helps you through life because setting a goal and sticking to it, will prove to you, you are far more capable of working harder than you thought. So, make your plan for the day, work at achieving it and earn that day, Make it yours!

CHAPTER 7
THE ROLLERCOASTER

In 1975, my life and health seemed to roll along smoothly and I soon opened a van and 4 wheel drive retail shop on Route 22 in Union, NJ. The business was great and I expanded into installing everything I sold. You could literally drive to my store with a stripped cargo van, new or old, walk through my store and pick out wall, ceiling and floor coverings, cabinets, lighting, windows, seats, alarm, sound system and seat configuration, or we could build you a custom sin bin in the back (basically a large bed). Then drive it to my shop across the street and within a few days, you would have a custom interior with windows, custom paint and all the bells and whistles. It was a great time to be in business in America. It may have been one of the high points of self-expression with American automobiles.

I soon opened a second store in South Jersey and my life was booming. I had pockets filled with money as I worked 18 hour days, and it was a real gift.

One night I went to a club called Dimples, there I met a great girl named Nicky. We became dancing partners and friends. One day she said to me "I have a sorority sister I want you to meet, she is perfect for you." That is when I met my wife to be. She was hot but not like the rest of the young ladies I knew. We danced, and within hours I took her to the back of the club where it was very quiet and I said these words, "Listen to me, I like you and one of two things is going to happen, either I am going to marry you or we will go our separate ways. In case we stay together, let's make a deal, never to lie to each other. Let's go dance." She was 19 and must have thought I was nuts, but I knew what I wanted and this woman was different. Lucky for me (for her, maybe not so much) I married her 10 years later. By the way, I never hear the end of the 10-year courtship even though it had a 1 year break in the middle.

Then one cold autumn night in 1979, I came home and sat on my brown sectional. I put my leg over the arm and relaxed. All of a sudden, my stomach felt uneasy and then it got worse. I noticed blood in the toilet that night and little did I know, but my life was about to change.

Soon I found out I had colitis. My mom died from ulcerated colitis that turned to cancer when I was 4. I started going to doctors and they assured me it was not life threatening and very manageable. I was told that 1 in 2000 cases of colitis turn into ulcerated colitis. Of course, mine did. Then I was told 1 in 2000 cases of ulcerated colitis turn into cancer, so do not worry, and of course mine did. This pattern continued with one disappointment after another.

Overnight, my perfect life was crushed. I was devastated. Lucky for me I had the support of a great family and a wonderful woman. For the first year of my disease I wasted a lot of time feeling sorry for myself. I continued to work, but I was no longer effective, I was just going through the motions. My doctors wanted to perform surgery to remove my rectum and colon and give me an ileostomy. One day my father talked to someone and he recommended a doctor at the Lahey Clinic (Dr. Crozier). My dad called the clinic and found out the doctor was at his fishing cabin in Maine, but the clinic took a message. The next day Doctor Crozier called. He said, "I have arranged for your son to come into the clinic and get care and I will be back in a week." Doctor Crozier stabilized me to the point that I could at least think again. The best doctors in the world will make time for their patients, because they care.

During the first 18 months of my illness I mostly sulked and felt sorry for myself, and one day I started to reflect on my life. I remembered when I was a young man just 19. I tried to leave the automobile industry and sell real-estate for a few years. I worked at Kings Manor Real Estate, and every morning I would go out and knock on doors to see if the home owner was interested in selling their house so I could list it for them. I said the same thing at every house, "Hi, sorry to bother you. I was wondering if you could help me. I am from Kings Manor Realty and I have a client who is looking to move into this lovely neighborhood." I tried to knock on 100 doors a morning.

One morning I walked up to this house that sat atop a cliff looking at the New York skyline. A beautiful woman answered the door and I gave my pitch. While I was talking, I looked over her shoulder and the house was filled with lovely young women. Just then a man in a wheel chair zoomed up to the door and said, "What do you want?" I told him and he said, "Come in and sit down. I like young kids that are hustling." I sat on the couch as he directed the beautiful girls. I stayed as long as I could and from time to time he zoomed over and talked to me. His business (I believe it was a modeling agency) was run from his house. When I walked outside, there was a white handicapped van and it had a painting of a man in a wheel chair. And it said something like Billy the wheels Shu—.

Later, I learned he had MS. Now faced with my own situation, I thought, what can I do that he did? Here was a man who could not walk and was destined to suffer and die before his time and yet he was enjoying everything life had to offer to the fullest. Actually, he was doing better than anyone I knew at the time.

If Billy could live such a life, I could at least improve my situation 10-fold, I thought.

I went back to the 2 rules I discovered as a young man. Rule #1: As long as you are doing what you feel like doing, you can never have what you truly want. Certainly, Billy, sitting in that wheelchair, had to force himself to do all he was doing. For me, clearly it was time to start eating better and exercising, stop counting my misfortunes and focus on my good fortune. Time to start using all the lessons I had the privilege of learning. I started doing what I did not feel like doing. First, I set up an exercise plan (boy I hate to exercise, even to today) and an eating plan. For some time my right hip had been hurting me, so I developed a plan to exercise the legs without impact.

When it came to cooking, I learned that what I thought was good food, was not. You know all the buzz words you see on TV like, organic, humanely-raised, sustainable, no hormones, heart healthy, whole grain, all natural, loaded with antioxidants. After diving into nutritional books, I quickly realized I had no idea of the value of healthy food.

I decided to hire a professional chef, educated in nutrition, to come into my home and teach me how to properly prepare food for the most nutritional value. After talking to a few, I ran across a macrobiotic chief.

Keep in mind, I am about 130 pounds and very weak. In comes this lady chef, who right off the bat made it clear she was the boss. Well great, I thought to myself, a person in charge. The first thing that was made abundantly clear to me was that I had to have a special carbon steel knife. Not a stainless-steel knife, but a knife with a carbon steel blade and a natural wood handle. I tried to reason out the rational of this, but it was clear to me I should go with it. I bought a great 7 inch blade kitchen knife to make her happy (actually I still use it.) Then we moved on to Miso and Nori seaweed soup. This is where I started to realize this lady was a little nuts, but like my dad always said, "Shut up, you might learn something." So, I did. It is very important how you cut the seaweed. If you cut it wrong, you would disturb the yin and the yang. And for goodness sake, never ever stir the soup counter clock wise. I made that mistake one night, stirring mung bean soup counter clock wise and I thought the world was coming to an end. She literally exploded and became upset. "You are disturbing the yin and the yang and the soup will not be good for you." I know my wife was in the other room trying not to laugh.

She reprimanded me a few more times that night, but we got through it. Actually, she came regularly and we got along well. In the end, I did learn a lot from her. So much so that I decided to go see the head of macrobiotics and get some firsthand advice on healing my severe ulcerated colitis.

There is a benefit from mixing the diet into a smart Mediterranean diet, but to isolate yourself in any restrictive diet, I feel is a mistake. The most important thing I learned from this experience was about beans and how to prepare them, as well as making healthy soups and using sea weed.

Beans are wonderful things and I recommend them, but you must take the time to prepare them properly. Especially because your system may be compromised. Azuki and black beans are my favorite, but I eat them all. Soaking a bean from 10 to 24 hours is not an option, it is a must. If you eat beans in the can they are not soaked, so your digestive system is dealing with compounds like lectins and phytic acids. These compounds are protection for the bean while it is in the field against pests and diseases, however they are not friendly to our digestive system. Soaking will help remove them. Soak your beans the recommended time (on package or internet) and then discard the water, rinse your beans twice and cook them to taste. Beans are loaded with nutrients and protein. I love black beans over a bed of yellow rice (I use turmeric to make the rice yellow, never food coloring). Then I plate it with finely diced sweet red onions, good quality olive oil and a few dashes of Tabasco sauce.

I cook my beans by first sautéing till soft and add diced onion, diced red bell pepper, garlic, sea salt, pepper and olive oil. Then add the beans, water and white wine, cook until tender and scoop them into a bowl of yellow rice.

To make great yellow rice fast use 1 cup of white rice, 2 cups water, dash of Mrs. Dash or other combined spice, 2 chicken bouillon cubes, ½ teaspoon of turmeric (an unbelievable anti-inflammatory). Cook recommended time.

Turmeric is wonderful, and I take it daily every morning and night. I take about a teaspoon. It has many wonderful benefits, but for me it is about controlling the inflammation in my body. I buy organic turmeric by the pound on line for about $10 to $20 a pound. For me, a pound lasts months.

Miso soup is tasty and great for you. The Asian countries have consumed it for centuries as a great detoxifier and probiotic. Miso is a paste made from fermenting soybeans, sea salt and rice koji. It has a great taste and I mix it with everything. I keep it simple, miso paste, small cut vegetables and wild small shrimp, chicken or beans. Also, never buy shrimp or any fish that is farm raised, it is poison. Nori sea weed, cut small, is also a great addition to miso soup.

My #2 Rule: You become what you think about all day long. It was time to start seeing myself in my mind's eye as the person I wanted to be. That picture was a man standing upright and in perfect health.

My new path was fraught with ups and downs. I did not rocket into a positive life style, but I moved forward every day with changes not always for the better, but overall positive.

While I was trying to go forward I worried about the baggage of cancer and what was to happen in my future. In these situations, thoughts will run through your mind. Why fight to get better when the cancer will get me anyway? Just relax and let my days pass peacefully. One day, when I was reading, I came across writings by Mark Twain. He said, *"I am an old man and have known a great many troubles, most of which have never happened."* There it was. I sat for hours after I read that, reflecting on my life, my teachings and my experiences. From that moment on I was no longer sick. I realized the cancer did not happen to me, for I am the subtotal of all I have learned, the people I love and care for, the people who love me. I am what I have made myself, etc. I am not my body. My body is a vessel I occupy. Taking better care of this vessel will strengthen it and improve my health and mindset.

Lucky for me I was always a people watcher. I looked hard at the lives of my friends and acquaintances. They had no real tragedies and yet they rode the rollercoaster of unsubstantiated highs and lows and led lives of mediocrity. They let daily influences blow their emotions from one hill to the next valley. Then there are the gifted, those who have everything, including great health. However, when I looked a little closer, I could see the shadows of the rollercoaster going by.

Does anyone have the perfect life? Well, I have come to realize there is no such thing. However, maybe, there is a close second.

To be healthy, is truly the greatest gift one can possess at any given time. Certainly, good health allows us to do more. But good health in and of itself does not guarantee you a perfect life. In fact, we all take our good healthy days for granted and let them go by unappreciated.

It was becoming clearer to me that I am not my body. Certainly, when my body was in pain and discomfort, it had the power to interrupt my appreciation of life, but it was not me. The separation of body and me, is now, and always will be, a work in progress, but a worthwhile quest.

During this period, I spent a lot of time thinking of how I allowed my body to destroy my life. The messages I received from my doctors, nurses and loved ones was to take it easy, relax, give your body a chance to heal. Of course their advice made perfect sense and so I did as directed and I realized I was once again my own worst enemy. The first time I ever heard those words [Sam, you are your own worst enemy] I was in second grade and Mrs. Stern wrote on my report card, "Sam is his own worst enemy." I remember opening my report card on the way home and thinking to myself, what does she think I am doing, hitting myself?

Although I started to improve my diet and exercise, I had no vision of where I was going. I was just trying to get better. One day while sitting in the living room gazing at the TV, I remembered 2 things that happened to me.

When I was young, my dog had major surgery and when he came home, he rested with a big cone on her head. The cone was to prevent him from licking his wound. The next day Duchess was up and running around, slowly, but never the less, running around. Duchess was not going to let the day go by. Duchess did not have the world telling her to relax and lay down.

One night I flopped on the couch because I had a runny nose, headache, and stomach cramps. All I wanted to do was go to bed and be left alone. The phone rang and I ignored it. Soon it rang again and again, but I did not answer. Once again it rang and I thought, it may be someone I care about that needs help. "Hi Sammy," it was a girl friend of mine. "What are you doing tonight?" "Oh, honey I am a mess. I feel like shit. I am just going to lay low tonight." "Sammy, Jane and I are at the Back Door (a local night club) and we were thinking about coming to visit you to have some fun all night long, are you sure we can't come over? We will make you all better."

I knew I could not do this, it had been hard to drive home from work, but things started to happen. In my mind's eye, I remember how much fun they were and how beautiful they looked out of clothes, one was a belly dancer and the other a dance instructor. I started to feel better and my nose started to dry up in a matter of seconds. All of a sudden, I was no longer leaning against the kitchen wall, I was standing in the middle of the kitchen and feeling better. By the time, they arrived I was feeling pretty good. Well, details of the night are not the issue, but it is a very fond memory, the point here is that we really are what we think about. Our mind has an impact on our physical wellbeing.

So, rule #2 of life is: "You become what you think about". I heard it said in many different ways, but the bottom line is, we are the keepers of our mind. We are in charge of the gate to our mind and if we let disabling thoughts in and fester on them, we become disabled. I still, to this day, meditate and visualize myself as a healthy strong man capable of caring for those I love.

Keeping good thoughts in my mind is hard for me. So, I keep a card with me that I will look at during tough days. The card is simple. It says: *"I am healthy, I am productive, I am happy."* I read it over to myself from time to time while in a relaxed meditating state, all the time visualizing myself in my mind's eye as a healthy prosperous person. When I am coming back from an occasional health issue, I made a deal with my wife to not coddle me. Don't let me feel sorry for myself. And never stop me from getting up and going, even if she knows I am wrong and should be resting. I know it is hard for her sometimes and sometimes she thinks I am crazy for going to work and pushing 12+ hours a day, but she backs me. Like I said, I got lucky.

You see, one of the problems is how can you tell if you are really in need of sleep and rest or if your mind is lying to you. The truth is, there have been a few times when I was not ready to get back to my life and all hell broke loose, but rest fixed it. However, most of the time I really was ready to get back into my life and getting back made me better, faster. One thing for sure, Billy the Wheels did not let his limitations slow him down.

I try to live by, *'the more you do today, the more you can do tomorrow, the less you do today the less you can do tomorrow.'* Often, I am in rough shape. I can get infections and internal inflammations and lose 10 to 15 pounds in a day or two. I feel terrible and depressed, but I have a rule. I can feel sorry for myself for 24 hours, then I put my hand in my back pocket and pry my ass out of the chair and start working towards the best health I can have. It is ok to give yourself a little time to get back on track, but after that, get up and fight. Believe me, your heart, soul, and body are begging to get better. Sometimes I have to start by just walking around the house, then the backyard, then the street, until I'm ready to go to the gym.

Being productive or fighting to be productive and getting busy with living will change everything. I can't promise it will be as much fun as the 2 girls that came over to visit me, but you'll feel a hell of a lot better.

There are so many great natural foods that are fun to eat and great for your body. Clams are one of my favorite. And there is no better way to eat them as clams in green garlic sauce. Clams are loaded with vitamins, minerals including selenium, magnesium, vitamin C, B12, copper, phosphorus and riboflavin's, a great protein source and low in fat.

Clams in green garlic sauce for 2.

Little neck clams are my favorite, smaller clams have little meat and too large and they are tough.

1. 36 clams, clean the shells well (Sometimes I take a brush to them)
2. One loaf of Panera baguette or other great French or Italian crusty bread
3. Bunch of fresh parsley, cut the stems off and discard them
4. 1.5 cup cheap, dry, white wine or cheap Chardonnay, my favorite is Jolina white cooking wine from Restaurant Depot
5. 2 tablespoons butter, ¼ cup good olive oil
6. 5 cloves of garlic
    a. Put in a blender, washed parsley, wine, butter, olive oil and garlic and blend until you have a green broth.
    b. Bless the clams (after all, they are giving up their lives for your health.)

    c. Put the clams in a deep pot with enough room for them to open up.

    d. Pour the mixture over the clams.

    e. Cover and turn the heat on high, once they boil down to medium.

    f. Cut the bread on an angle and set aside.

When they open, they are done. Plate them in a bowl and scoop out the juice. Now throw the clams out and dunk the bread in the juice, just kidding, enjoy. Great for an appetizer or a main course.

Clams casino is also a fun way to enjoy clams. I like to switch it up a little to keep it as healthy as possible. (For 2)

1. 36 littleneck washed clams opened and placed on a low cooking sheet pan, you can go to YouTube for opening instructions. Some people will steam them open and then fill and broil them. I prefer to open them raw.

2. Into a food processor: 2 carrots (cut up) washed, not pealed, half red onion quartered, 5 cloves of garlic, half a zucchini (cut up), ¼ cup Italian bread crumbs (optional), ¼ cup good olive oil (add a little water if the mixture if too dry) and pulse until the mixture is a very course puree (like oatmeal). Spoon the mixture on to the clams and fill the shell, sprinkle garlic granules / sea salt mixture on top and broil for 10 minutes or until light brown. I mix my garlic sea salt; I buy granulated

garlic and mix it with a fine sea salt, about 3-parts granulated garlic to 1-part sea salt. Always use a good sea salt, never use table salt.

I also like to juice, there are a lot of juicers on the market. I have an Acme juicer that I bought in 1980. I use it a lot and today and it still runs like the day I got it. I have other juicers in my home in Florida and they cannot compare to the Acme. Carrots are my staple, but I also add beets, celery, cucumbers, apples, wheatgrass, pears and kale to name a few. Just mix it up and have some fun. A glass of a good juice every night is a good way to tell the cells in your body, that you are coming back.

Good foods are a large piece of the puzzle, but without exercising and controlling your mind, you will not benefit to the extent that you desire. Meditation is so important. We are bombarded with stress just from day to day living, and if you are dealing with an illness, it is compounded.

There are so many simple ways to meditate. Being allergic to pain meds, learning to meditate was essential for me. I simply relax in a comfortable chair or I lay down in a quiet place, close my eyes, take a deep breath and on the exhale, I say to myself that my feet are completely relaxed, after my feet, I do the same thing with my legs, torso, chest, arms, head and neck and face. Each time I breath in and out I feel my body part fall away from consciousness. I visualize myself calm and healthy.

I mediate for 10 minutes, all the time seeing myself calm and happy. Sometimes I visualize myself standing strong and healthy. Meditation has always been a work in progress. I usually stop doing it when things are going well, but in times of trouble I rely on it to keep me focused. It is certainly a piece of the puzzle. I recommend keeping it simple, so you can do it at the drop of a hat, almost anyplace.

CHAPTER 8
FINDING MY SURGERY

Every day was a struggle to keep my health together. I was taking drugs to slow my bowl down and cortisone orally and cortisone enemas every night to slow the bleeding. Arthritis kicked in and every morning I had to literally drag my feet to the bath tub and soak them in a hot tub to get them going. I could not get off the medication, but I was getting a little stronger and once again working 12 hours a day. It seemed if I kept a very strict diet and took the medication I could maintain some sort of a life style. I was not kidding anyone especially myself, it was evident I could not go on like this; I knew that if the drugs didn't kill me, one day the cancer would.

To make things easier, I bought a van and built a small bathroom in the back and a dinette that turned into a bed, for when I needed to lay down; it gave me flexibility. I could now go anyplace and not be in fear of not having a bathroom.

My research led me back to juicing. I knew a little about juicing because of my friendship with the health food store owner when I was kid. I read all the medicinal properties of aloe vera plants, so I found a company in Mission, Texas that grew aloe vera plants and they would ship the entire plant to you, root and all, and they were about 5 feet tall. I started buying them and planted them in the house. I filleted the leaves and juiced them. Over the course of a day I would drink ½ of a quart of fresh aloe vera juice. Over the next few years I flew in organic Poi from Hawaii and goat extract from the mountains of New Zealand. I visited vitamin companies to see their processing and settled on Solgar as I liked their processing and the cleanliness of their facility. I drank juices regularly, including ½ a quart of cabbage juice. I ate raw vegetables and fruits, cooked seaweed and beans and rice and of course always stirred them properly (just in case my macrobiotic chef reads this). I was stabilizing, but still weak and sick.

I had charts of everything I ate and everything I tried, like aloe vera and cabbage juice, I methodically took my supplements and juices every day, several times a day and never introduced any foods that had the potential to irritate my bowl. My diet consisted of whole foods. Poached eggs for breakfast with oat meal. For lunch and dinner, I ate broiled, steamed or baked fish or chicken with brown rice, steamed vegetables and a focus on vegetables from the crucifer family, known for their ability to fight cancer: cauliflower, broccoli, boke choy, brussels sprouts and cabbages. I made every meal myself with only the freshest organic foods I could find.

I was obsessed with the idea of regaining my health. I had a nurse come to my house every week and draw blood, then I compared the reports week after week to see if the things I was doing were actually helping to improve my health.

My charts and methods were not influenced by how I felt, they were facts. After many years of researching results of so called miracle products, I came to the conclusion that every wonder food was a waste of time. Don't get me wrong, it is imperative that you eat well, but that perfect Mediterranean diet without sugar and wheat is the overall answer to getting strong. There is not now, and never will be, one food that will make a large difference. It is about collecting pieces of the puzzle.

Living well is a work in progress and you must fight to find the pieces of the puzzle and then be responsible enough to make them part to your life. Then and only then will you move forward, with some kind of consistency.

As for the blood test successes, I was able to keep an eye on my white count and with anti-inflammatory drinks, like turmeric powder, cucumber juice, pineapple juice, carrot juice that was freshly made in my kitchen and consumed immediately, it helped to keep my inflamed colon somewhat in check and mitigate the infections. Never forget, if you are taking a juice in a bottle or can or powder, it is not much more than flavored water. All the life-giving benefits that we really do not fully understand have been boiled out or killed. When you hear that if you take this drink or pill, it will give you all the nutrition of a long list of vegetables, most of the time it is not true.

From time to time I would fall apart and end up in the hospital. Luckily, I had a great local doctor to work with (Dr. Clemente). If I was suffering blockages and needed to get to the Lahey Clinic, he was there for me. I would need to go to the local hospital and get hydrated as quickly as possible. The problem was that every hospital has to run all their tests to protect themselves however, when in this state I would not have time to go through that process. Dr. Clemente would call the hospital as the ambulance was driving me there and tell them, "Just do whatever this man asks for, he knows what he needs." I would arrive at the hospital and be hooked up with the fluids I required. Soon as I was stable, I'd be in a car and heading 280 miles to Lahey Clinic.

Over the years I discovered that I was allergic to any kind of pain medicine. I could take it for the first 4 hours, but another dose and I started to hallucinate and became violent. Onetime we tried different and new pain meds when I was at the Lahey Clinic. The first dose went well and 4 hours later the second one was also fine for about 2 hours. But then out of bed I flew, I pulled all the intravenous out of my arms and the chest feeding tube as well. Blood flowed from my arm and chest as I ripped my hospital gown off and went running down the hall yelling "I got him, stand back." I ran back into my room and slammed the door, jamming my feet against the door, not allowing anyone to come in.

Through the years, different doctors would try different pain meds, but it all ended up the same. From time to time I would have to go to the hospital and get more treatment to stabilize my bowel. Once I came home from the hospital with lomotil to slow my bowl activity down, but the narcotic sent me off again.

I was taking several medications, so it was difficult to know what was causing the hallucinations. Finally, I was having a lot of bowel activity and bowl pain, so I would take another lomotil as prescribed. That sent me out of bed, down the stairs and crashing into the front door, fighting with the hallucinations again. Lynne called my father and together we walked the streets of Madison for hours, trying to get me stable. I needed to be off the drugs and pain meds.

Through the years of frustration, something good was happening that would prepare me for finding my future treatments. I was learning how to get information from doctors and institutions. It took a while, but I realized it was not always the doctors who were the problem with medicine, more than not, it was the patients. Fact is, we go to the doctor to have them fix us, plain and simple. We do not go to be part of the process. If a doctor really sat you down and told you the truth about everything, he would have few patients. It is our fault that the profession is so guarded. I learned to ask questions, and to listen, then go home, research my condition based on the information the doctor gave me. Then take my problem to another specialist and ask more questions, but this time more informed. Do this a few more times and I guarantee, you will find a doctor who says to himself, "This person is willing to take control, be responsible for their health and I want to work with them." Then, and only then, will you really be on your way to your best possible outcome.

I really think most doctors enjoy having a patient who is informed and disciplined. When I mean informed, I mean, you understand your situation from his point of view.

One day I was home and something new happened. My skin turned bright red and I was going crazy itching from head to toe. I was not sure what was happening, so I ran to the bathroom mirror and sure enough, my skin was red. I did not know what to do and for about 10 minutes it consumed me. Luckily it always went away, but when it attacked, I was out of control. I learned that heat and dehydration made it worse, so in the summer, if I was driving, I kept the ac on high in my van and if I had an episode I would pull over, go to the back of my van and strip all my clothes off until it subsided. One winter day I was very weak and dehydrated, a recipe for my skin to flare up. My skin turned red and I was on fire. I started to lose control and then I remembered cold helped. I ripped off all my clothes and ran out the back door. Through the door

I went and jumped into the snow and rolled around. In seconds, the itching was gone (If you by chance were one of my neighbors, let me say, I apologize, I was the nut rolling in the snow with no clothes on. Thanks for not calling the police.) These episodes never lasted long, thankfully.

I spent a few years trying to get my severe ulcerated colitis under control. By this time I had gone to see many nutritionists and I realized it was time to look at surgery. I could no longer live on drugs and bouncing from 125 to 140 pounds.

I started to research ileostomy operations and I came across an operation where they removed all of your colon and your rectum and construct a small pouch inside your abdomen out of your small intestine, and then construct an opening in your stomach wall (a Kock pouch). Basically, you had a pouch in your abdomen as a reservoir and you inserted a small tube and drained the pouch. This sounded very interesting, I learned that the pouch seemed to perform well, but the valve they made in your stomach wall failed regularly.

I found operations where they removed your colon and removed all the mucus tissue around your anus and pulled your small intestine down and hooked it up to your rectum. This worked, but the frequency you had to go to the bath room was not reasonable.

My search went on for months from every corner of the world, there was no internet at this time so it was a difficult process. One day I called a doctor in France because I read that he was doing something different with the Kock pouch. We talked for a while and he told me to call Sir Alan Parks at the Royal College of Surgery in London. He said that they were doing just what I was looking for. At the time, Sir Alan Parks had performed 80 of these surgeries on patients. Soon I made friends with the nurses and assistants and over the next year, they agreed to let me talk with patients. I jumped at the opportunity. I sent gifts and thank you letters to the nurses and assistants. I even spoke with Sir Alan Parks (a great guy). Within a year I had a real good idea of what I wanted. There were S pouches, modified S pouches, W pouches and some J pouches. I kept a record of everyone and as the months passed, it was clear to me I wanted an S pouch, that was over 30 years ago, but today I think would have opted for the J pouch. Over time it has shown that the retention capabilities are about the same and it uses less of the bowel in case it has to be removed down the line.

There were different results from patients with a short limb to the rectum from the pouch to the anus and long limbs. Soon I had a handle on all this. I drew the pouch and limb as I wanted it. I knew the Kock pouch worked, but the valve failed and the pouch fell sometimes. I knew that the anus could control the pouch because of research I had done on the small intestine being pulled through the anus. I had a pouch and valve together in one operation.

Then I looked at what would speed the recovery up after the surgery. It seemed that the only thing I could find was a small section in a book by 2 great people at the forefront of research at the time, PHDs, Durk Pearson and Sandy Shaw. They talked about pantothenic acid (B5) as a precursor to acetylcholine. Acetylcholine is a molecule that acts as a neurotransmitter. People who suffer a traumatic experience like surgery, have a dramatic drop in the level of acetylcholine, hence their bowel activity or peristaltic action, which is a series of wave like muscle contractions that move food in the bowel, stops.

So, I had my S pouch, the length of lower limb and my vitamin B5. Soon I found a way to get B5 in injectable form. Now the search was on, all I had to do was find a colon rectal surgeon who would listen to me and work with me. I started setting up appointments with the most noteworthy of the bunch. I forget how many said to me "This is experimental and will not work or last," and they scoffed at my drawings and findings. Soon I found a team in NY who had performed many of these operations. Off I went and although they were very well versed in the operation, they found my information to be more of an invasion of their superiority. All I wanted was someone who knew what they were doing to put my life back together by removing my diseased colon, but they did not get that. I did manage to get friendly with the doctors and the nurses and over a short time I gathered statistics, some from conversations with the nurses and doctors and some from talking with patients. Within about 4 months I discovered that they had a huge failure rate. The funny thing is at that time, they were rated #1 in the USA for this operation. Most of the failures were two things: 1, picking the wrong patient for this operation because it does take some adjusting to over the first year or 2, patients had a lot of infections that required more surgery to correct the problem, (sloppy surgical procedures.)

I kept looking. One day I made an appointment with a surgeon at the Lahey Clinic at the suggestion of Dr. Crozier (my gastroenterologist at the Lahey Clinic). I sat with Dr. Coller and his assistant Dave. I told them my thoughts and they looked at one another and did not say much. I stayed for some rectum testing to see if I was a good candidate and then we all had a meeting. Dave handed me my notes and drawing. Dr. Coller then said the following beautiful words "Sir Alan Parks is a friend of mine, we have worked together and I agree with your conclusions. I would be glad to do your surgery, however I cannot use your injections of B5. I cannot use anything that does not come from our internal pharmacy." Later I had a company ship it to the hospital pharmacy via a pharmacist I met and we did use it. Soon I booked the operation and off I went. It takes a special doctor, like Dr. Coller to hear his patients.

By this time my hip was hurting a lot, but I never really gave it too much thought, I felt I had bigger fish to fry. The recovery from surgery was slow and interesting. Because I could not take any pain meds, so I walked the halls in the hospital all night. My plan was simple, grab my stand full of bottles on wheels and walk until I could not stand any longer from exhaustion, then I would sleep. Soon I was home and control was all in my hands. I was due to see Dr. Coller in 30 days.

I had an arsenal of nutrition and exercises ready so I could get back to the old Sam. I fought to gain weight and get strong. 30 days later I drove to the Lahey Clinic in Mass. for my follow up appointment. The nurse called my name and I went into see the doctor. I was waiting and then I walked to the door of the examining room and looked up and down the hall. Down the hall came Dr. Coller and he glanced at me and walked by. I said "Doc, Doc it's me, Sam." He looked and walked into the room with me and said, "I cannot believe how good you look. I did not recognize you." I had gained 25 pounds in 30 days. I knew from his expression I was on my way.

Soon, Dave (Dr. Coller's assistant) called me from the Lahey Clinic and asked me if I would talk to some other patients who had the same operation and share some nutritional information with them, and of course I did. I called it dietary management for Parks procedure. Not sure what happened long term, but I like to think it helped some.

All of this would not have been possible had it not been for the fact that I am married to a most amazing woman. We need support, but with support comes responsibility to those who love us, to be as healthy as possible so everyone can enjoy as much of life as possible.

Your quest will be met with obstacles, but every time you overcome one, you become more informed and stronger. Talk to doctors, patients who have been in your situation, research treatments, supplements, whole foods and keep your focus on who you will become.

Remember, your goal is to cure your situation or learn how to live with it well and have a full life, always looking for improvement. You should always be working towards getting better. Never stop fighting and growing.

So, exercise, eat nutritious meals, meditate, do your research, talk to your doctors and above all, stick to your plan, never waver.

CHAPTER 9
THE FULL MOON

Being a people watcher for most of my life, I have noticed people doing the same thing that they believed was the best path, only to fail, and then continue to behave in the same manner time and time again. Regardless of their frustration, they never seek a better plan or change.

When I was recovering from my first surgery and balancing my new pouch, I was getting stronger and becoming more myself. I was now 160 pounds, working 7 days a week and rebuilding what I had lost, which was almost everything.

It was a fall night with a very light rain, cool, but not cold. There were few leaves left on the trees and it was a full moon. Throughout my life, a full moon was troublesome for me. It seemed that during a full moon, I was searching for relief of some kind from something.

This evening was no different as I sat on the front porch of my house in Madison, NJ, hoping to find that relief. My hands hung from my knees and the blood had all but stopped running from my knuckles. I recounted the events of the last hour in my mind over and over again and once again, as so many times before, there was no rationale. The moments of violence were instant, uncalculated, and so encompassing of my every fiber as many times before.

Sitting on the front step of my home I gazed across the small country street, where leaves rustling gently down the street helped to calm me. I noticed the full moon peering through a large leaf stripped tree across the street, and thought to myself, (*there it is again, my ghost, my enemy, my old friend who was filling the sky with brilliance. Maybe what they say is true, full moons bring out the crazies*).

Earlier during this night, I was closing my store and loading things in the trunk of my car. It was an especially bright night thanks to the light of the full moon. As I was bent over, loading the trunk, a man shoved me and I hit my head on the side of the quarter panel trunk rail. A fight started and lucky for me he had little skill. It was over very quickly. My dad boxed and taught me a little. Actually, I had little skill, this man had less. Later I learned the guy that attacked me, had mistaken me for someone else.

I gathered my thoughts and proceeded to my car, with my hands dripping with blood, I drove home.

On the short trip home, I recounted the times in my life when this uncontrollable anger consumed me. I remembered when I was 14 and a full moon kept me from sleeping. The next day in school, a bully had been beating up another smaller kid. I do not even remember the start, but within minutes, he was on the ground and asking me to stop. Lucky for me he was just big with no skills at all. To me, it did not matter if I won or lost. There were just times of the month that I was nuts and vulnerable to my rage, coincidentally, all around full moons. I became more violent as I got older.

Funny thing, I never got hurt and I never felt any pain, it was like I just had to get on the other side of something bigger than me. Once on the other side, the calming began and all was normal to me again.

When I was 4 and my mom died, my dad moved us to a house across the street from his laundromat and shoe store. The house was located in Springfield, NJ. We lived right on Morris Avenue, almost the last house before the commercial buildings started.

When I was a small child, up to my teens, I would wake in the middle of the night, emotionally out of control. Some nights I could not shake it and I ran outside into the full moon light and walked until 2 or 3 in the morning. Sometimes I would play with my cars and trucks alongside the house. I would walk the street back and forth and always felt safe because there was always a lot of night light from the full moon and somehow it comforted me. Eventually I would become exhausted and go in and fall asleep. One night when I was 15, I woke up about 2 miles from my house with about 6 inches of fresh fallen snow on the ground as I walked on railroad tracks. I had on a tee shirt and pajama bottoms and wet socks. I was wet, my arms, head and body were covered with snow. Once again, I was standing in the light of the moon and felt no pain or fear. I realized I was in Summit and I knew how to get home. Needless to say, when I got home, I was a frozen mess, but I was ok. I never woke my father or sister. Somehow, I was not alone and now on the other side of my haunts and back to normal.

There were times when I was told I was with people late at night and I had no memory of it. I had a small ski boat and kept it in Bricktown, NJ at Johnson's Boat Basin, about 50 miles from my home. One summer day I was with my friend Tony and our girlfriends. We were water skiing and enjoying the day. We were watching this race boat go back and forth in the bay. A guy driving the boat stopped and waved. I looked around and saw no one else so we all waved back. The man drove over to our boat and said, "Sam, hey Sam how are you? Thank you so much for pulling my boat out of the swamp." I said, "No problem. I almost forgot, when was that?" He said, "A few nights ago, I'm Andy. Thank God it was a bright night or you would never have seen me." I had no idea who he was, but apparently that night I drove 50 miles to my boat at Johnson's Boat Basin and went for a ride. The good news was he had a racing boat and he took us for a ride.

When my friends and I got back to the boat basin, I asked Mr. Johnson if he remembered me taking the boat out a few nights ago and he said, "Of course. You must the love the night, because you go out a lot." I guess I have been there on other occasions.

Then there was the guy who would come and steal my car and put miles on it and put it back on the street in the same place. Well, this was so confusing to my dad that we actually waited at night for the guy. You guessed it, the guy was me.

So here I am, a grown man sitting on my front porch stairs, trying to calm my anger. The evening was chilly and the full moon on the other side of the neighbor's tree was bright. I remember the bushes were a little over grown and a small leaf branch, rustled by the wind lightly brushed against my face, a nice touch of reality for my troubled soul.

As I sat on my porch staring across the street, something grabbed me. I was looking at 2 visions of the moon through the tree, the one in front of me and the one in my past. Suddenly memories of my past flooded my body and soul. The memory of maybe the most tragic evening of my life became clear and vivid, sending shivers down my back and somehow giving me relief. It was a mixture of information and emotions scrambling vividly in my mind. My hands that were cut and battered, started hurting as if to say, "it is ok to be human." The urge to cry was overwhelming as my past rushed in.

I was 4 when my mom died. I was not fully aware of all that had happened, but I was certain something bad had happened. Shortly after she left the house, men brought her back, only this time she lay in a box and never moved. Back then, it was not unusual for the viewing to be in your home. That evening my dad told me to play outside. We lived in the country and outside at night was safe. He walked me outside, knelt down and hugged me. He said, "People are coming over for a little while and you should play outside". He hugged me again and was very sad. I walked around outside playing and people came and went. Some of them ran over and knelt down and hugged me and then whispered to one another as they walked away. There was a row of my favorite trees in the front yard and they had these long beans on them. The beans were so long that I picked one and made like I had a sword. Soon, I got tired and walked across the driveway to the front of our house. I sat in the tall grass and watched the wide open front door. I could see my mom's coffin and people walking around. It then became clear that something really bad had happened. There were people crying and hugging my dad.

People parked all over the driveway and they had no problem walking up to the front of the house because Dad had hung a bright light bulb high in one of the bean trees. As I sat in the grass I remembered the light breeze blowing the top of the grass, rubbing against my face as I watched the front door. Things started to set in. From where I had been sitting that night, I could see across the dirt driveway, down the sidewalk and straight into the front door and see my mom lying still. The side walk was lit by that one light bulb high in the tree. For a long time I sat, looking at the front door, at my mom inside, still, as my dad greeted those who arrived.

Now, as a man sitting on my front porch, staring across the street, staring at the moon, a leaf gently touched my face, as a full moon was about to bust out of the sky with brilliance. Just on the other side of a leaf stripped catalpa tree, loaded with long beans gently swaying in the wind silhouetted by the moon, I sat, overlaid with my memories of my mom laying still in our house, a bright bulb hanging in the bean tree, and unexpectedly, I was free, free from the torment and anger of the full moon.

That moment was the beginning of a lifelong search to understand who I am. That night served to give me the wisdom to know, **that I do not know**, but must keep searching, reading, watching life, and never sitting in judgment.

I used to be trapped in a constant behavior and justified it with rumors and fables of a full moon's power. I learned once again that if we are trapped in a position within our lives, it is because we stopped growing, reading and researching.

I have been asked many times how I have succeeded in life in spite of all that has happened to me. One thing comes to mind, I tell everyone, **"My secret is that I know that I do not know."** I question everything in my life and seek for a better perspective to see where I am at any given time. Solid knowledge is the only way you will be able to stand back and see your life for what it is. I have found that old books are my greatest friend. During my first cancer I picked up a book that was an interpretation / translation of writings by Marcus Aurelius from the battlefield. Very difficult for me to read, but what I found was intriguing to me. I discovered that things have not changed. Many of the observations of people, society and politics were the same as today. We have a tendency to think we are superior and smarter than yesterday's society. I have come to learn that maybe, as a society, we are dumbing down.

From Marcus Aurelius, I learned that success is simple, not easy, but the formula for success has always been the same. "Our life is what our thoughts make of it." Jesus said, "All things are possible to him that believeth." The list of important writings throughout history all mention that it is our choice, that we can control our thoughts and our life. Maybe the single most important thing is to fight to be in control of our thoughts, as the thoughts in your mind at any given moment, are who you are at that moment.

When I was a young man I read a book written by Dorothea Brande, *Wake Up and Live,* written in 1936. For me, at that point in my life, it was not filled with many new thoughts, but the information was handled differently and driven home harder. I recommend reading it. She talks about failure and success differently and with more intensity than others and emphasizes controlling our thoughts. My only criticism of self-help books of today discussing the power of positive thinking, is that they may be worried more about being politically correct, and do not stress the fact that, a positive outlook is useless without, dedicated, uninterrupted hard work. Nothing happens without great sacrifice and one's single-minded goal.

We have a tendency to think we, us, our time is special. Read enough about years gone by and you start to feel ashamed that we have squandered knowledge and worse yet, ignored what was learned and offered to us.

My recommendation is simple, get up 15 minutes early and read something about self-improvement that is at least 50 years old. You only have to do it every morning for the rest of your life, so it is a part-time job in the big scheme of things. After a few months of reading the old books, you will realize they are talking about today, with the bs removed. I have several translations of the meditations from the battlefields of Marcus Aurelius. When I go to my home in Florida, I go out in my small boat late at night and I love to drift in the back waters and read them.

Life is indeed a rollercoaster, but with a plan for success you can lessen the dips and the highs to have a more level life style. Fueling your body with a solid Mediterranean diet, exercising and meditation, prepares you with a positive mind to research and fight any problem that comes along. When I know I am heading for another surgery or inevitable hospital stay, I prepare. I lift heavier weights and try and increase my cardio. Without question, if I go in stronger, I heal quicker and get my life back on track much faster.

I like that my good days, are just that, they are mine. I earned them, by following a disciplined plan, and I cherish them and enjoy them. Working towards better health, a better life, relationships, will benefit you in more ways than one. Never take any of it for granted. Own it, work at I, be responsible for it.

CHAPTER 10
A VISION

So, things were on an upswing. I gained weight and I was on the other side of my first big operation with its ups and downs, and I was learning how to live with it, and maximize my life style. A few years prior to this I had noticed a pain in my right hip. I ignored it because ulcerated colitis seems to emphasize arthritis and I figured, I had bigger fish to fry.

Well, it was getting worse (the pain that is). I finally went to the doctor and after x-rays, I was diagnosed with avascular necrosis. The right hip (femur head) had a dead triangle in the top of it and was degenerating. The x-rays showed that the head was jagged and rough looking. They told me it was in 4th degree collapse, not a good thing.

As it turned out, the disease, avascular necrosis, is often caused by steroids. And I was taking a lot of cortisone and hydra cortisone to control the internal bleeding over the years while I researched the best surgical option. My first reaction was, to be mad at the pharmaceutical companies and the doctors. Then I looked at it objectively and realized whose fault it was, it was mine. I had made the decisions to search out my best surgical option and to stay on the steroids.

I went to 8 doctors (specialists) for consultations and after each consultation I researched what they had said. Pretty soon I was getting an understanding of the disease from a layman's point of view. Every doctor I met with gave me a better understanding of my disease and after research, I was able to ask the next doctor better questions. With better, more informed questions, came even more information. Out of the 8, 6 doctors urged me to have the hip replaced immediately. Some contended that I could damage the upper socket and need to have both upper and lower replaced, instead of just the lower.

It is too easy to sit back and say, these doctors did not care about me and had operating rooms and their bank account to fill. There may be some truth to that, but I really think it goes much deeper. They are in the business of healing patients that do nothing for themselves. They are focused so much on trying to do the right thing for their overwhelming disconnected caseload, that they really are not looking for alternatives to the gold standard they work to. Because most patients do not change their lifestyle, medicine has prepared for that. The medical profession is governed by so much litigation and misinformation propagated by the pharmaceutical industry, that it is restricted from looking outside the box. They are fighting to keep us alive the only way they were taught because of our lack of participation in our own health. Today, more so than ever, doctors have no alternative / nutritional training. Why should they? We are not participating in good health. Think about it, does it make sense for a doctor to be trained in something the patient will not do?

We are to blame. If we are told to quit smoking, stop eating greasy foods, stay away from sugar and flour, packaged food, processed dressings, exercise more, why ignore the advice? Instead, for those not actively involved in improving their health, drugs are prescribed as the only remedy. What else can your doctor do?

Back to what I said before, it is your health problem, not the doctors. If you sit in front of the doctor and have the attitude, fix me, I am all yours, what do you expect? You have to convince the doctor by your actions, not your words, that you are going to discipline yourself and be an active part of your recovery. If you are diabetic and overweight, let your doctor see you are making an effort by losing weight, exercising and eating properly. The things you do, the effort you make will send a message to him (I am working with you on this project, how am I doing and what else can I do?) Get involved. If your doctor does not respond to your changes, find another who wants to get involved.

At this point in my life, I have a cool cane and I am getting around and researching the disease. It seemed that there was no answer, but there were a few doctors doing different things. I found a doctor in Japan that was cutting the femur head off the leg bone and rotating it 180 degrees and fastening it back with screws. The theory was, that it would grow in and one day after the healing, you would walk on the other side of the femur head that had not died; sounded interesting. The statistics in Japan were around 85% success. The problem was when he sold the idea to a few USA doctors and they performed the operation with him, there was a 100% failure.

My first reaction was how is that possible? After a lot of prying, I learned that many studies from abroad are fudged. They are not even close to being accurate and there is a very good reason. If a doctor abroad can come up with a cure or procedure for anything that is different, and proves it, he will most likely get an offer to come to the USA and work at a major hospital.

That is not to say that some great medicine does not come from around the world, but you really have to be careful. The case of the rotating hip, it was misleading, it never worked.

However, in the process of trying to prove that the doctor in Japan had a great idea, I ran into the osteoblastic cell. It seems there are cells that generate bone growth. In a nut shell, we have all heard about the astronauts losing bone mass because there is no gravity in space, so they don't need to bend their bones. When you bend your bone, there is an electrical current generated and it lays down bone cells.

I was looking for some way to regenerate the bone cells in my femur head. I found a doctor in Maryland who was working on the osteoblastic cell related to the deer's antlers. A deer's antler is the fastest growing bone in the animal kingdom. He was actually taking the cells from a growing deer's antlers and placing them on the deer's leg and getting growth. The research did not help me directly, but I learned a lot.

His research led me to a doctor who at was making a small incision in patient's thighs and placing a battery in their leg with 2 electrodes drilled into the femur. The intent was to electrically stimulate the growth of bone by duplicating the electrical energy generated naturally by the body. I was interested, so I read all the information I could. I found out that there were very limited results. Still thrilled with the idea, I made an appointment to see the doctor who was head of the surgery. When we met, he looked at my x-rays and we talked for a while. First, I showed him my research and told him why I was so interested in what he was doing. I showed him my information regarding why the procedure was not working. He said, "Sam, come with me." I followed him out of his office and through a class room. As we walked through the classroom I noticed human legs on tables. We got into his office and he closed the door, he sat in front of me and said, "Sam, this process helps. It is simple and it gives the patient another year or two, because they think it is helping, but you are right, it has not been successful. Tell me what field of medicine you are in?" He thought I was in the medical profession and that is why he was honest with me. Can't thank him enough for his honesty. Had he not been honest with me, I may have missed the hip saving study, just around the next corner. Because I got involved, he shared a lot of information with me. Remember, always get involved. I know we are all so busy, but here is a secret. Sell your TV and you will have more time.

All of my life I heard that carrots help your eyesight and they are the best thing you can eat for your eyes (not totally true). I wondered about this. As it turns out, in World War II, the English were destroying German planes at night and they spread the word that it was because their pilots were eating carrots for increased night vision. In reality, it was a new type of radar they wanted to keep a secret from the Germans and throw the Germans off track. The myth about carrots continues today.

Studies can easily be groundless and slanted to a result they desire. It depends on who pays for it and what their goal is.

I ended up looking into veterinarian medicine, particularly a study where they were trying to save valuable horses that had broken a leg.

That led me to a company that was in the middle of a small study to fix my exact problem; regenerate the femur head. I called and they sent me to their doctor for evaluation. They got back to me and said, "Sorry, you cannot come in to the study because we are only taking people in 2nd degree collapse and you are too far gone and in 4th degree collapse." To make a long story short, I called them every day for 6 months and one day the guy said, "We will make you a deal. We will give you a machine, but you cannot be in the study and you have to stop calling." I said to him, "We are halfway there." He said, "What do you mean?" I told him "I work a lot and I want a machine for my office, as well as home." They agreed. To tell you the truth, I know they gave me the machines to get rid of me.

So off I went with another project. I went on crutches and eventually practiced to build myself up physically to make the crutches part of my body. I could run on the crutches without touching my feet on the ground.

I never touched my foot to the ground for over a year. I did exercises to bend the bone and not stress the femur head to activate the osteoblastic cell. I ate a diet friendly to bone growth, with supplements from places like New Zealand, where they had bone meal from the goats of the mountains. My earlier research told me that L-arginine and L-ornithine would stimulate my glands to make natural growth hormones.

After my surgery to build my pouch about a year ago, I could not get off steroids. If you are taking steroids, your body will stop naturally producing the .78+- milligram of steroid. To get off steroids, it is a gradual reduction and some people never get off the last 1 milligram because their natural production never returns. Consequently, they go into adrenal shock. I had this problem and could not get off the last 1 milligram. I had a great book by Durk Pearson and Sandy Shaw, *Life Extension* and its companion. It informed me about taking supplements and what to do nutritionally to stimulate the pituitary gland to produce growth hormones to get the adrenal gland to start producing steroids. I would be wrong to say this alone solved my problem because no one could really tell, but the fact is, I finally got off steroids 100%.

For me, the lesson is about being involved. I wonder if our body and maybe even our individual cells are listening and watching to see if they should make an effort to get better or just keep withering away. I think they are naturally positive, but need a leader, so as not to not lose their way.

One day I put the crutches against my van and jumped in the driver's seat. My wife came out of the house to talk and I pulled out of the drive way and I forgot the crutches. They stayed in the driveway. 60 miles later I met a builder at a house I was looking to buy, but I had no crutches. I knew I would have only walked around for a few moments, but I would be breaking the promise I made to myself to beat this disease. I told the builder I could not get out of the van. I drove all the way back home (60 miles), got the crutches, and drove back again.

If you are going after something, you better be 110% focused or it will elude you, no exceptions, all or nothing. That is not to say that you cannot start on the right path, get distracted and still be successful, but you better realize, you just went back to square one and are starting over. Building your health is like building a basement wall, you cannot leave one block out of 5000 blocks needed or forget to put in the 1 pound out of 2000 pounds of cement required, do that and the wall will fall apart.

I live by a simple rule: Complete the task and stay focused. Here is an experiment. Sit in your kitchen at the table, now sit in the chair 4 feet away on the other side of the table at the same time. Fact is, you cannot. You can only do one thing at a time. Every fiber in your body wants to pull you to a single goal. Help it stay focused with your one priority. Whenever someone applies for a job and tells me they are a multitasker. It scares the hell out of me. Give me the guy who jumps on one project and rides it until it is 100% finished.

I have learned that our body is listening to everything we do, everything we think and speak. Say or think out loud that you are sick, and you feel worse. Tell yourself you are feeling better, and you begin to. Eat junk and your body says, "This person is not serious about helping me get better," and down the rabbit hole you go." The fact is, if you know it is bad, and you know it will not help you, that alone starts the flow of chemicals in your body that are not conducive to getting you better. We don't really understand this fully, but there is little question that a person taking control of his recovery feels better, and when you feel better, there are chemicals released into your blood that will help the building process. Nurture this process and be proud of your dedication, you will only benefit from it.

Today, I have my same hip. Within about 18 months of getting my semi- conductor impulse generators, I was walking normally. Today, some 30 years later, I am still walking on my hip. I attribute this to the fact that I did not waver in my determination and dedication to improve my condition.

My research of the different types of hips available at the time was extensive. So extensive that a surgeon in a local hospital asked me if I would talk to patients he had before they submitted to surgery. I was glad to share what I had learned. You see, he had his hip replaced and it was problematic. Funny how good things follow good actions. I was on my way to Hayward, California to a factory I owned and sitting next to me on the plane was a man who worked for the largest manufacturer of hips. He spent his life visiting doctors and lecturing on hip replacement. I told him of my problem and he told me the wonders of his company's hip. I talked to him about my research and he seemed very interested and he said, "Sam, do yourself a favor, put off getting a hip as long as you possibly can, they last from 4 hours to 5 years, unless you are not active." That was 30 years ago, so I am not sure of the numbers today, but from what I hear, I think the numbers are close to being the same. Participation puts information in front of you; it is the difference between being proactive and passive.

As for the study regarding my semi-conductor impulse generator, it failed. I am convinced that it did not fail. The truth is the people in the study failed the study.

I was lucky to be on a plane in Huston and loading my machine into the overhead compartment when I noticed people were watching me. When we arrived, a guy walked up to me and introduced himself. He was from the company that made the machine and we shared some stories. It seemed that other participants were of the mind that they did not care if it worked, because they felt a quick fix would be a hip replacement. He said they are not using crutches as they should, they are walking on the damaged femur. Trust me on this, there is nothing simple about surgery. None of them took other steps to help the process of regeneration. I know there is no way to prove why I still have my hip and living a full life with it. I believe it was the combination of the food, exercise, nutritional supplements and my mind set, along with the coil

I slept with and sat on in my office. Whatever it had been, it worked.

Believe in your recovery. Imagine yourself getting better, stronger, healthier. Visualize it every day. That kind of mindset can go a long way towards improving your health. It also helps your self-image and makes it more likely that you will also stick to a lifestyle of good foods, a regular exercise routine and meditation. A person with a single-minded goal who never varies 24/7 is a missile that cannot be stopped.

CHAPTER 11
OWNERSHIP AND POSSESSION

From time to time I suffer from blockages and the doctors have asked me to come up to the Clinic and have some tests done to see exactly what is going on. I am one of those people who develop scar tissue after surgery (called adhesions). I always resist a little, but soon I give in and go. By this time in my life, I have had so many things inserted into my bottom, that it no longer embarrasses me. It once terrified me, but one day it changed. On this life changing day I was in the hospital getting a barium enema (oh boy, my favorite), I have had many through the years.

The nurse comes in to give me an enema to clean me out. She says, "Hold it for a while and then use the toilet" "Ok, no problem". Next, I go to a waiting room and find myself sitting there with about 6 patients, some in arm chairs and some in wheelchairs. This is the holding area to further embarrass us. We all know what is about to happen to us and all are embarrassed. We are looking away from one another's eyes and remain silent. Suddenly it hit me, what the hell, we are all in the same boat. So, I held my gown closed and stood up. I said, "Hi, my name is Sam and I am about to go through those doors and they are going to stick a probe up my ass, now the good news is, I am in a hospital and not on an alien space

119

ship, so things are looking up already. Anyway, they are going to fill me full of white stuff. I don't like it, but it is my deal for the day. The way I figure it, you are all probably going to be going through the same thing. Having had this several times, any questions?" Bingo, the place came alive and all of a sudden we were telling stories about the last one we had gotten and laughing.

In I go for my barium. This change in attitude felt good. I crossed the line of tragedy to humor. My doctor sticks his head in and says, "Hi Sam, just passing, how are you doing?" I don't know where it came from, I am sure I must have heard it before because I am not that clever, but I guess I was moving along emotionally about the process. I said, "I am doing fine, but my ass dropped in for a milk shake and I thought I would come along." He closed the door and walked away. The technicians were stopped dead in their tracks and I remember thinking "who said that?"

There is something about letting go of your anger and embarrassment. It empowers you and gives you some freedom. Needless to say it is hard to feel positive when in pain, but I have found that pain is best handled by a well-rested body and mind. I know it is hard to rest when in pain. I have found that it is one of those things that you just work on until you are on the other side of it.

It is a funny thing about fighting through a blockage. For me, I walk, and during the walks that last all night, I grow as a person. It is then and maybe only then, that I am single-minded. I am not thinking about anything else but getting through the night and blockage and not letting the pain get so great that I black out and crash to the floor. In that state of determined focus, I find me, my worth, my soul is visible to me. I know that there is more to beating a disease than in the medical books. We are truly responsible for ourselves and have internal powers just waiting for us to release them.

Some nights, and there have been many, I find myself walking in pain and laughing to myself about how in touch with every fiber of my body I am at that moment. It is those times when I realize how empowered I am, how so much of my life is truly up to whether I listen to life or try and tell life what to do. Listening to the life around us and behind us (human history) is so important. During these moments I am reminded of my beliefs and my discoveries. I think about how I started winning a better life as a younger man. This is the most important thing I ever adapted without any option or wiggle room.

I never underestimate the power of possession and ownership. Being in control of your health, your business, your future and every other aspect of your short stay on earth is all about possession and ownership to a large degree. When I am walking late at night by myself, reality of possession and ownership is so clear. Fact is, when I become stable and join my normal life, the importance of ownership and possession fades, if not held onto tightly.

I listen to parents guiding their children and hear the reverse of what should be related. A simple thing like two siblings fighting and one hits the other. The first thing I hear parents say is, "Why did you hit your sister?" At that moment you are being taught that, if you can come up with a reason for your actions, it is not your fault and you will not suffer consequences. We have been trained by parents and society alike.

It stands to reason that you and I have a subconscious defense mechanism that immediately moves blame and gives up possession and ownership of anything that does not fly. We do not even think about it, it is just how things are.

Years ago, I was building commuter vans for Chrysler and my partner Dom and I were invited to go to the factory and tell the panel of engineers what they needed to do to make the vans more conversion friendly. There was a long table with about 12 of us sitting at Chrysler headquarters. The lead person from Chrysler said, "Why don't we start by going around the table and everyone can introduce themselves and talk about what you've been doing." It was clear to me that these people were highly trained and very accomplished.

Soon we were talking about a few problems with the van they were producing. The lead guy pointed out that one of their concerns was a problem they had and he started pointing fingers at those who were responsible. Within minutes, seven of the members got up one by one, stating it was not their department and had no knowledge of the problem, and left the room. It was a mass exodus of grown men running from claiming responsibility. The lead guy mumbled something and we continued. Clearly, they were also highly trained in not being responsible for things that did not work.

Therein lies the beginning of the problem when it comes to regaining back a healthy life. If you believe it was not your fault, you may not work as hard as you should to correct things. Feel responsible, take ownership and then, work your ass off to improve things.

This is truly the key for all of us in every aspect of our lives. It sucks sometimes, but it works.

Don't throw this book away until you rethink this over for a few weeks and maybe try it. I figured this out about 10 months after my first cancer.

"I believe everything is my fault." I adopted this belief and it has given me full control. It has given me a great family, a vacation home on an island, a great home, friends, businesses and maybe most important, it has saved my life. It may be the most important item on the table when facing anything in life.

"I believe I cause everything that happens to me." If I am standing on a corner and get hit by a bus, it is my fault. It was my decision to be on that corner, I could have been more aware. I could have stood closer to the building, etc. I do not care about the bus crossing my path, that was the bus driver's decision and his responsibility, it was mine to watch him. My cancers and other diseases were 100% my fault. I could have altered the current outcome, but I did not. Basically, I violated one of the two most important rules in life; *I did what I felt like doing during my life, as opposed to what I should have been doing and caused my situation.* I made the decision not to be informed about nutrition and necessary precautions that may have prevented certain outcomes.

I am not saying thrust the blame on yourself and feel guilty. Accept your situation and assume that you are the responsible party so you can fix it. If you are not to blame, you are powerless. Say to yourself "this is my fault," and start looking for ways to correct your situation. Own the situation and you will have the power to fix it and work towards changing your life for the better.

Claiming responsibility empowers you. Jump in and take action and your actions multiply. I believe we were meant to resolve all that comes our way. True, maybe you might not be able to change the outcome, but you can change how you live the journey. 'I AM RESPONSIBLE.'

Fixing a problem has a starting point that is pivotal. You can either start by knowing it is not your fault and your path will be fraught with anxiety and anger or you can jump in knowing you caused it and only you can fix it. This path is filled with pride and emotional reward. I am not saying it is easier, but ultimately it is the only way to fill your life with happiness and security knowing you are controlling your life.

I remember sitting in my house in 1982 (at the time I was about 125 pounds, down from 170 because of my first cancer) and discovering this about myself. I was confused and lost at that moment. My recollection of that day is that I was reading meditations from the battlefield of Marcus Aurelius and what he said was "All things that were his, were his to change." It hit me like a hammer and I felt lost, ashamed, saved, confused and enlightened. I thought to myself that I had been wasting my precious days on earth by playing the blame game.

At that moment, I told myself everything is my fault. Since I caused it, the logical next thought was, I can fix it. From that moment, I started real research and dedication to find answers.

It was the beginning of my new found ownership.

You must own it, to fix it and then work to change it. Can't fix what is not yours.

If I sound a little positive as a result of being sick, well it sucks, but I realized something, I am a better man sick, than I ever was healthy.

Dr. Coller said it best. One night he stopped in to see me when I was in the hospital and he said. "You've got to get off the medical merry-go-round."

There is no down side to eating right, taking proper supplements, exercising, researching your options and taking advantage of them. And never forget, search for humor in your situation, laughter is one of the best medicines.

Faced with the responsibility of helping yourself, you need a daily plan. When I am first recovering from a devastating situation and coming back, I keep my meals simple, and bland. I write my daily plan going forward on a paper and I stick to it.

Regardless of what you are coming back from, a simple and basic diet is better. The chances are great that your digestive system has been compromised by trauma, medicines and or antibiotics.

Phase one of coming back:

Breakfast:

1. 2 eggs poached or scrambled.
2. In a blender, blue berries, banana, one scoop of protein powder that contains a probiotic, acidophilus capsules, tablespoon of good cod liver oil, 1000 mg capsule of vitamin C, capsule of Vitamin D3, 1 teaspoon of turmeric and a little water.
3. Cup of herbal tea, never canned or bottled juice.

Lunch,

4. 1 can of skinless boneless sardines in olive oil. Don't turn away from this lunch. 1 small can of sardines has 22 to 26 grams of protein, lots of omega fatty acids, calcium, iron and potassium and minimal calories for the value.
5. A good slice of whole wheat bread.
6. A small portion of pasta with a little butter.

Dinner:

7. Roasted chicken (maybe not the skin, it can slow digestion), with a little sea salt (never use table salt). Or broiled flounder, cod or salmon, (never farm raised fish.) You can safely flavor up salmon without too much effort. I like to marinate it in a plastic bag with

olive oil, lemon juice, chopped and crushed garlic, bay leaf, and sea salt.

8. Roasted or steamed vegetables, I like to roast my veggies, in a shallow baking pan. I place sliced onions, eggplant, tomatoes, zucchini, asparagus, carrots or parsnips. Lightly sprinkled with sea salt and garlic granules and drizzled with olive oil for 15 to 20 minutes at 350.

9. Close the night out with a glass of freshly made carrot juice with a teaspoon full of turmeric. You can buy 1 pound of ground organic turmeric on eBay for about $10.00.

10. Avoid all coffee, regular tea and any soft drinks, alcohol and chocolate.

Phase two, when my body starts to respond to healing, I keep the same breakfast with 2 scoops of protein powder and I add strawberries to the smoothie.

11. My lunch and dinners are similar, but I have more choices and I add lean meats cooked well. Use only good cuts of meat, as it is easier to digest meats that are more tender. You can also cook roasts and chuck cuts for a long time and braise them to the point that they are falling apart. I will cook myself a roast and refrigerate it and later slice and make sandwiches on a good slice of whole wheat bread. Don't be afraid of making your own breads. With a little trial and error,

you will be amazed how great the house smells when you are baking bread and of course you now have full control of the grains in the bread.

12. I add salads and mix it up so that my salad is as tasty as it is inviting looking. Your body will respond to meals that taste good, look good and are nutritious. I bring the cabbages into my diet, cauliflower, brussel sprouts, broccoli, steamed and roasted at first and then raw in my salad. Big salads are key. Make big salads with lemon juice and olive oil topped with blackened chicken breast strips or sautéed shrimp (wild only). I love to put in a frying pan, chopped sun-dried tomatoes (that were in a jar of olive oil), crushed garlic, sea salt, red pepper flakes (optional), paprika, a good splash of dry white wine, cook for 5 minutes, drop in cleaned shrimp and cook for a few minutes. Place on top of your salad or over real brown rice. A great meal topped with a little parmesan cheese. Salad dressing will always be lemon juice or apple cider vinegar and a good olive oil.

13. It is now time to eat beans, and please don't buy them in the can. You must soak beans overnight and then the next day wash off the harmful chemicals your body does not want to deal with.

14. I always start my day with my smoothie and finish with my carrot juice, changing up other vegetables in the juicer.

15. You don't have to cut out all the fun foods, but just be smart about what you eat. Once a week you can have fun. I buy baby back ribs, cut them into 2 or 3 rib sections. Steam them until they are falling off the bone, for 2.5 to 3 hours to break down the fat and connective tissue and then cool. I baste them with my favorite barbecue sauce and place the ribs in a plastic bag and refrigerate overnight so the barbeque sauce sets in. Take them out of the refrigerator and broil them or grill them. Baste them 2 or 3 more times when turning them, caramelizing the barbeque sauce.

I started steaming meats to remove the fats and break up the connective tissue so the meat was easier to digest and came up with some great dishes. At my family picnic, I will go through 30 pounds of ribs, my family and friends love them. Ok, not the healthiest dish, but you need to have some fun.

When you are coming back, you must eat healthy: fish, lean meats, chicken fresh vegetables and fruits, and good whole wheat bread (try making it).

When your body starts to respond and you begin to feel healthier, you will appreciate the meals you make and the steps you are taking to improve your situation. Make a simple plan that includes: eating healthy, exercising, meditation and taking ownership and this will be the beginning of a better life. And stick to it. This is your only life.

CHAPTER 12
REACHING OUT

During all of this turmoil, researching to find the right course of action, surgery and dealing with   avascular necrosis and the constant blockages, my business life suffered as well. I had four foreclosures being filed, banks running from me like I had the plague and my savings was zero. I lived in a beautiful contemporary home on Barnegat Bay with 40 feet of windows facing the bay and wetlands. However, the house was in foreclosure and every part of my financial life was crashing down around my wife and me. My health was stabilizing, but from time to time, after being worn down, I'd have to build myself up again.

It was a Sunday, about a month before Christmas, and I was resting in the living room and acting distraught. Lynne said, "Are you ok, what is going on?" For a while I remained silent and then told her I needed rest. As the day wore on, I said, "This is the first year in many years that I cannot give food to the less fortunate in town during the holidays." We were both silent for a while and then she left and went upstairs.

For as long as I can remember, just before Christmas, we would contact the town and get a list of people in need. Every township or county has a list of people who are having a tough time. During the holidays they will have a difficult time putting together a holiday dinner. When I get the list, usually 100 to 150 families, my wife and I buy boxes, put in a large frozen turkey, cans of string beans, corn, sweet potatoes, canned juice, cranberry sauce, stuffing mix, rolls and a tin of cookies, basically enough food to feed a family of seven. Before Christmas, at one of my buildings, we stage the set-up, packing and delivery for that morning. My dear friend Dom and my office manager Barbara head it up. A friend of mine, Pastor Clem Salerno, will show up while we are packing and bless the people and food. Usually deliveries are finished by noon with the help of many of my friends who volunteer their time. This year we were broke and losing everything, there would be no Christmas dinner to help those in need. It was a sadness that ran deep in my heart. I had let so many down.

After a while my wife came downstairs and said, "I have one credit card with money left on it, that I was saving for the next time you have to run to the hospital. Here, use it to buy the food for the people who are in need." I looked at her and said, "Honey, we cannot pay our bills. We cannot buy food. We are losing all our properties." She looked at me and said, "Honey, I know we have a mess on our hands, but somehow you will get us through this, you never stop fighting. These people need this food to make their holiday better and you need to give it to them to be who you are. You will get us through, you thrive on the fight".

I told you she was special. Once again, we made Christmas special for many who were struggling.

About 3 months after that, we were still in a financial mess. Actually, it had gotten worse. All the banks were screaming foreclosure and even though I had offered several options and begged for more time, they were coming at our properties hard. It was another Sunday and we were sitting at the kitchen counter. My wife hands me a letter, smiles and walks away. I took out the letter from the already opened envelope. It read like this. "Dear Mr. Casternovia, I am 45 and crippled from arthritis and my mom is very sickly. We live in Brick Town and the bank is taking our house and the township is threatening us because the taxes are so behind. You have helped us every year with our Christmas dinner and made it so special, would you help us with this problem, we cannot lose our home." It went on, but you get the jist of it, someone in need of help, apparently with no one else to contact.

Soon my wife walked in and said, "What are you going to do?" We both laughed because we had so many problems we could not even help ourselves. I said, "I will call her." I called her and she explained her situation in detail. I told her I would set up a meeting with her bank and go with her to try and get them to reset the mortgage and help her. I was going to go, but I could not get my banks to help me. This was clearly not my area of expertise.

I made an appointment to meet the president and the vice president at her bank at 9am on Tuesday. Mary was to meet me at the bank and my plan was to go in and plead her case, but actually beg them to work with her. I arrived 10 minutes early on a late winter morning with blowing and freezing rain. I walked up to the door and it was still locked. Just then I saw a woman get out of her car and try to walk across the sleet covered parking lot. It was Mary (this was the first time we met in person) and she was in worse health than I had imagined. I greeted her and we knocked on the glass door. Now 7 minutes to 9. The banker came to the door and I said, "We are here to meet Mr. Johnson and Mr. Blake." The young lady said she will get them and scurried away before I could say, "Please let us stand in the lobby". Seconds later the president arrived at the door and said, "Your appointment is for 9am, come back then." "I know we are early, but Mary is ill and cannot make it back to her car and we are both getting soaked." "That is not my problem; we will let you in at 9." And he walked away. 5 minutes later we were let in. Standing in the lobby, soaked and trying to get out of our coats, I said to Mary, "Do you trust me? Do you trust that I will not let you down?" "Yes, I trust you." she said. We walked into the board room with 6 people ready to discuss Mary's mortgage. A young lady said, "Mary sit here." I said, "Mary, don't sit, we are not staying that long." Then I turned to the group and said. "I don't know how, but I am coming after every fucking one of you in this fucking bank, and when I get through with you, you will kiss her ass to give her the mortgage." I turned to Mary and said, "Let's go honey" and we left.

Now I had a problem, I had promised. I did upper and lower court searches (something my bankers did on me) on everyone in the bank. I investigated every person in the bank, and let me tell you, dig far enough and everyone has baggage, or you can spin seemingly innocent things to sound bad. I met with reporters, newspapers and anyone who would listen. Soon I had a story that no bank wanted public. As it turned out, the bank had its own problems with the government. The bank was now occupied with government officers watching their every move. I met with the bank's president and the government officers and we made a deal. About 12 months after I started, the bank forgave the rest of her mortgage and I got the township taxes forgiven.

I used everything I had learned from helping Mary to deal with the banks that had been coming after me and within 24 months, all of my properties were on solid footing and I was going forward nicely.

Had I turned my back on Mary, I would have lost everything. There is indeed a natural order of life. It is all around us, waiting and hoping we use it. You cannot touch it, see it or conjure it, but you can earn it. Your actions evoke the goodness which is your allotment. I am a religious man, I do not go to church every Sunday, but I feel close to God. Do I make mistakes? Hell, if I did not make mistakes, I would only have to work 2 hours a day instead of 12.

We are more than what we see, we are body, soul, spirit and we come to this place we call earth all connected to one another. It makes sense to me that our lives are reflective of our deeds and commitments to others. I have always called it the 'Natural Order of Things'. It cannot be denied that it exists. Look at any successful person and you will see they committed all to their task. I know some of my dearest friends have told me, and I have read that God knows all and knows every hair on our heads. I do not doubt that, but I submit this. I believe it is a natural order that God has set up. I believe it works for all, regardless of intention.

It is undeniable that if you hold one task before you and work on nothing else, it will be yours. I have learned if you do not reach your goal, it is because you may not have been focused.

I was blessed with the gift of having been asked to help Mary, and I know it.

My wife walked into the living room and gave her last bit of money to a very weak, sick, man. Who does that? Lynne knew if she helped me be the man I once was, I would help others and the circle that governs us would continue.

Sit someplace quiet by yourself for a while. Do it often enough and you will one day realize you are not alone. I have a home on the west coast of Florida. Occasionally when my health permits, we vacation there. When my family goes to sleep, I get in my little 15 ft. boat and head out into the back waters. I turn off the motor and drift. In the back waters, it is inevitable, in a short time, after all earthly possessions and influences leave me, I feel as if I am with other powers I cannot explain. I never feel alone and always come home a better man.

I think losing my mom when I was 4, made me begin to look to the heavens for contact with her. When I was young, I had a favorite star, I would swear it was her. So, I have always been open to the possibility of greater powers, which has let me see many options in life.

If you struggle for better health, keep a sharp eye open to see the needs of others. Helping others whenever you can, is a test to see what kind of person you truly are. Your reward may only be the warmth you feel while resting, knowing that you made a difference, but that in itself, should be enough.

When I first had my pouch in 1984, I was doing very well and I worked with many patients who had my same operation. My goal was to balance their pouch with food, supplements and exercise. I learned quickly that working daily with different people in search of some balance, was as helpful to me as well. My recovery plan was constantly reinforced, and helping others kept me focused. Every evening I went off to bed thinking about my conversations and the problems other individuals were dealing with. Helping others just became part of my lifestyle.

A mother calling you to thank you, telling you that her daughter is no longer afraid of an accident that would embarrass her and now able to resume her life, it is enough fuel to drive you forward for a long time.

The value of being humble and compassionate cannot be measured. Never forget, life is a circle, reaching out always benefits everyone involved.

CHAPTER 13
GETTING LOOSE

I have been sick now and dealing with this illness for most of my life, actually as long as I can remember. I am allergic to pain killers, so from time to time, life gets interesting. Through the years I have dealt with my health in many ways, trying to find a way to still be a productive member of society. I read everything I can find on pain management and being positive. One day I realized that I am too attached to my body and its medical whims. The constant rollercoaster ride is very disruptive to my personality and business. I thought about separating my body from my mind on occasion, but this time, something was different.

One night I was dealing with blockages and walking the floor for hours. It was a beautiful winter night and the back yard was covered with fresh snow. I put the flood lights on and when I walked from the great room through the kitchen and into the rear foyer, I could look out the more than 30 feet of windows into the white wonderland that was my back yard. The lightly falling snow was soothing. The pain began subsiding, the chance of passing out from the pain had passed and I was moving to the inevitable discomfort stage. Not a big deal, but certainly limiting my activities for a period of about

2 to 3 days. During that time, my bowel heals itself from all the ballooning and stretching from the blockages.

Relief was mine. I knew I would not be able to sleep, but resting was possible. I set fire to a pile of wood I had in the fireplace and sat in my recliner looking out the 12 ft. X 10 ft. great room window. The heat from the fire radiating out across the room warmed my body as the backyard flood lights washed the branches of the evergreen trees that were gently holding the powdery snow. It was mesmerizing at the least. The pain in my bowel was no longer surging with the movement of the peristaltic action, instead, the blockage passed and it was a constant low throbbing, a good stage to be in.

As I lay there, a calmness came over me, I was no longer consciously feeling my body. My thoughts were of other calming moments in my life. Like being alone in the woods late at night and early morning, sometimes with my dog Duchess, where as a young man, I found myself in touch with my soul and aware of the gifts that were mine to relish or squander and the heightened awareness to recognize the difference. As an older man, unable to walk long distances because of the avascular necrosis, I turned to the swamps and back waters of the west coast of Florida. Lucky for me I own a place on the west coast of Florida right on the water. Now, having a family, their security is always on my mind. Knowing I would want to be out at night, I picked my second home very carefully. You will probably think I am nuts, or maybe that my ship has sailed, but here is how I picked my family retreat. First, it had to be a place everyone in the family would love, after all, it is a vacation home. Second, it had to fit our needs and it had to be safe. I found 14 miles of islands with a bridge on each end going to the mainland. I purchased our home at the 7 mile mark, so if anyone was looking for trouble, they would have only 2 ways to get off the island. Additionally, it is 7 miles to the bridge either way. As a result, crime in the middle of the islands is almost nil. This allows me to disappear at night into the back waters.

Late at night I take my 15 ft. boat and drive to a place in the back waters, crossing the flats and into corners of the world where, at that hour, you are alone. On those very calm nights, I head out in the Gulf of Mexico until I can no longer see artificial light. In these places I escape my body and life and indulge myself in thoughts of being one with my soul. Here, there is no need to defend myself, my loved ones or my holdings, no reason to trouble myself over building an equity base for my loved ones, just empty space that is being filled with an awareness of my soul. The part of me that is truly part of the earth, heavens, past and future and mine to ignore or invite in, soothes my tired body and assures my mind of its potential.

Lying there in my small boat, I reflected on past issues with my health and the battle to recover so many times. I recalled a conversation I had with a sweet old lady in the health food store in Summit, NJ when I was just a boy. One day she reached overhead behind her, straining to pick out a small book with a dustcover that was well worn. She rubbed her hand over it as to clean off the dust and said to me, "Your headaches might not be something that will pass, but read this book, it may give you some information to escape the pain." I tried to pay her for the book, but she insisted it was a gift.

I read sections in the book several times and tried to meditate, but without success. Then one day while alone at night, I realized that I was calmer, and I applied what I had learned. The darkness around me was the piece of the puzzle that had been missing. The deep love I had for the woods at night, coupled with the information I had so dearly struggled with to absorb, came together. Meditation never eliminated my headaches, but it helped.

Now, many years later, I realized I was unknowingly using the night, the darkness, the solitude and meditation to get me through tough times.

One day I searched the entire house for the old book, but it was nowhere to be found. A short visit through meditation sites on the internet and I found a simple meditation procedure very similar to the teachings of the old book that I had as a kid. At different times and for different reasons, the ability to enter the meditative state is sometimes challenging.

To this day I still must work hard to get to where I want to be. Some days I am fully relaxed and in control in minutes, while other days it is a battle to get under control. I think that may be a good thing, because we tend to put more value on something we must work for.

Today, meditation is a part of my life. It guides me through dark moments, heals me, removes me from my body and physical discomfort and instills in my mind that I can win any battle put before me.

I have learned that I am not my body. My illnesses, my discomfort are not part of me. I am an entity, the subtotal of my soul, that which was granted to me, holding energy, knowledge and goodness, past, present and future and the subtotal of everything I have created, learned and of course, those that are dear to me. My body is another entity that allows me to function on this stop in the cycle of continuance. My journey could not be fulfilled without my body at this moment in my time, but it is not me. It is mine to maintain and care for, but it is not me.

Having separated myself from me, I started referring to my body as another entity. Something I do on a daily basis for my benefit. It occurred to me that thinking and living this thought may allow me to stop being involved with the sicknesses that plagued my body. My wife caught on quickly and soon we talked about my body as if it were a car needing service.

When I have been in trouble, she has actually said to me, "Honey, you need to get your body up to the clinic and get it checked out." It helps that she is a little nuts also.

The separation from the entity that gives me presence on this earth, has allowed me to avoid the rollercoaster of daily living, or at least minimize the highs and lows. Sure, there are times when functioning is difficult, but I try and keep to myself and not let the world know I'm in discomfort. One night I was out in the back waters in the very early hours of the morning with a small head lamp reading the meditations of Marcus Aurelius. In these readings I came upon something that was so fitting for me that night. He said, that when you are home and not feeling well, you should not linger in your pajamas, if you do not feel well and guests are coming, rise, get dressed and do not burden your friends and family with your illness, it is your illness, do not inflict it on them. It is your responsibility to add to their spirit, not diminish it. I try to remember this in times of stress and be less of a burden to others.

Those words have echoed in my mind for years, now they help bolster the fight to be everything I can be. I fight as not to burden others and I fight to not limit the lives of my loved ones. So many times I see a couple where one is healthy and fit, while the other is virtually killing themselves by eating bad food and not exercising. In some cases, they have an illness and do nothing to minimize the impact the illness has on their life. All the time they are also destroying the life and future of those who love them.

The entire thought process lets me step back and see what my body needs. At this point it is as if my body is my car. I own it, it gives me trouble sometimes, never really runs great, but I can still shine it up and make it look acceptable. Keep changing the oil and putting new tires on it and let's see just how long I can keep it running.

Think of your body as your greatest gift and pay attention to its physical, emotional and psychological needs. Our body is a sensitive machine and when neglected in any way, we pay for it. Be sure you are putting the right food and supplements into it and give it exercise regularly. Go on line and type into the address bar "simple meditation techniques" and you will have your pick. Keep it simple. If you start out small, it will turn out to be so much more in the long run.

CHAPTER 14
REAL HOPE

Throughout our lives opportunities cross our paths, sometimes they come in the form of tragedies, good and bad encounters, illness and sometimes they are just passing moments that we have to grab at and look deeper into. Twice in my life I have been witness to something that turned my head in a direction that has contributed to every aspect of my life. As a very young man, I always wanted to know something. Can anyone find that center and invoke their inner power to succeed? Can a person, not programmed as a child by surroundings to succeed, turn that around? Do we have the power to turn our tragedies into victories, even if we never have before and why is it that so many people seem to rise in victory seemingly effortlessly, while others, similarly motivated, struggle in every aspect of their life?

I was lucky (thanks to my dad) to feel a need to pay attention to life and watch and learn. More than anything, my inquisitiveness taught me something that I feel is one of my greatest assets '**I know, that I do not know**', and I spend countless hours looking for the right answer, humbly and without prejudice.

The search for answers to handle life's struggles was jump started by accident when I was a young man, working for Springfield Garage. I noticed many immigrants and natural born Americans coming in to the shop for truck repairs and repainting. It was not long before I noticed that there were men with little command of the English language who had businesses that were doing well and then there were others born in this country who had a truck, but their business was not so prosperous.

I talked to all of them when I could. From time to time they came in for tune ups, oil changes and repairs of body and mechanical. As we became friendlier I asked more personal questions. Soon I had a bag of questions directed at gathering specific information. I learned over a few years that it was typical for immigrants to come to America with a mental picture of where they were going to be in 10 years. Growing up in their country, they heard year after year about relatives who had come to America and became rich. They heard about the opportunity that was here in America and night after night they dreamed of coming to America and making their fortune. They heard stories of uncles who had built a business, owned a 2-family house, a 4 family and a big house for their own family. Every story programmed them to believe in their hearts that their dreams could be reality.

It all seemed to make sense, but still I had questions. One day I was talking with an older man from Italy and during our conversation I found the answer that solidified my belief in a simple single-minded goal. He told me of his boyhood dreams of owning a 2 family house, 4 family house and a great home for his family, and all built by his own business. A story he had heard from his parents and relatives sitting at the dinner table in Italy. I asked him how long he had been in America. "I have been in America for 42 years and this country has been good to me. I built my one family house 20 years ago." My first thought was that he built his one family home he resides in and then continued working and saving and built the 4 family or 2 family. Soon I learned that by the time he was 40, he owned a 2 family, a 4 family, and the one house he resides in.

Instantly I had questions. "If you built all that in 20 years, why did you not continue to build more properties? Certainly, by the time you had all those properties, you had equity and could have continued to build."

He shrugged his shoulders and said, "That's what I want." He left in his new truck as happy a man as ever I saw.

This showed me that a single-minded goal, ignoring distractions, works. In 20 years, he built a small fortune against incredible odds and after he was financially sound, he never went any further for the next 20 years. Soon, other stories followed the same path.

This changed my view of becoming successful. I now had proof that goals do control our life, so much so that in the face of success, with opportunities at one's fingertips, it may be difficult to see them. The only question was how to program my life and mind to take my soul forward to the next level. Progressing through my life, trying to stay single-minded on my goal was a struggle. There were times I thought to myself "if you are not raised with a single-minded vision that is burned into your heart, it is hopeless." Through the years I achieved more and seemed to be able to stay on course with some degree of frequency with victories being more common, but it has been a slow process.

Many years later I was working in my van shop when Dan walked in and looked at the selection of high back seats I had on display. He said to me, "Can you put 12 of these in a van and make enough room for an aisle?" I responded, "Of course I can, that is what we do." I really had no idea what he wanted or how I was to do it. He left and the following week he came back with others to look over the seats and a new Dodge van. I assured him I could do what he requested.

I drove the van over to the shop and started welding metal frame boxes to attach the seats to and bolt them to the floor of the new van. It was difficult to do, but we completed it. The customer liked it so much that within a short time we were the largest commuter van builder on the east coast. In 1997,

Entrepreneur Magazine chose us as Entrepreneurs of the year for all of NJ.

My health was rolling up and down, mostly due to my 14 hour a day schedule and the inability to balance my water and electrolytes, but I was about 150 pounds and working every day. The phone rang one day and it was the same man that introduced me to the commuter van business. Dan had a third-party commuter van business and was a hard pushing, very smart businessman. Through the years I learned a lot from him. He said, "We have a great opportunity to get a very large contract with the Palo Verde Nuclear Power Plant." I soon learned that Dan had agreed to supply the Plant with 100 commuter vans in just a few weeks. In my usual fashion I said no problem. Dan ordered 100 vans from Ford and we started staging the build out in NJ. Shortly we were ready to send 18 wheel box trucks on the long trip from NJ to Arizona, filled with our supplies, tools and material. When the trucks left NJ, Dom and I hopped on a plane and flew out to Phoenix, Arizona. We had 2 of our employees with us. As soon as we hit the ground, we went to the dealership and arranged for the dealer to deliver the trucks to the power plant. At the power plant, they gave us a large building to work in.

These vans were empty. They had no walls, ceilings or floors, no seats except one driver seat and no rear air conditioning. We were to install a plush carpet floor, foam padded cloth walls and ceiling and 15 custom high back seats, all with overhead reading lights and individual air conditioning vents. Bottom line, when we finished, they were custom interiors that looked like the first class section of a jet.

Prior to coming out, we placed ads in the local paper for help. Gus (one of our employees) started the interviewing process. We needed about 30 employees.

When we got back to the hotel later that day, Gus told us that no one called about the job. The next day all 4 of us drove out to the power plant. We set up manufacturing stations and started building vans. Our hope was that when we returned to the hotel that night there would be many phone calls from people looking for work. Unfortunately, when we returned there were none.

The next morning, we were up at 5am and heading out to build vans. This pattern continued for another day. In 2 days, we built 1.5 vans. The temperature had to be 100. The 3rd day and Dom and I are standing in the desert looking at 100 vans parked in orderly fashion, waiting to be converted. We were tired, and not sure what we were going to do. Dom who was 6' 3" looked down at me and with a very sad face, said to me, "I am going to be here for the rest of my life" and he walked back to the building.

There was little I could say to ease his concern. That night we arrived back at the hotel about 10 p.m. I was watching the news which showed pictures of acres of people who were homeless and sleeping in makeshift tents made from old tarps and such.

I said out loud, "That's it, tomorrow we go to the homeless shelter and pick up a truck load of workers." I jumped out of bed and ran down the hall banging on Dom's door. "I got it, I got it. Tomorrow we will have all the employees we need, see you at 5am."

The next day we showed up at the shelter and after some verbal maneuvering, we had a truck load of workers. Out we drove to the power plant. We made it clear no one could come if they had been drinking.

We showed up with about 15 guys jammed into a van. We started setting up stations and teaching individual teams how to do their particular job. Everything was jigged so it was easy work if you had worked with your hands before. We set up rules. If you go to the bathroom, you hustle or run. Walk and I will tell you once, second time, you are no longer working here. I ran to everything and Dom and I were the bench marks to hit. First day was tough, but we did find about 10 good workers. Second day, the good ones showed up with friends that knew the pace at the shop and were ok with hustling.

Lying in bed that night I remembered that I always wondered if anyone could be an incredibly productive person if they were not preprogrammed by circumstances. Thinking of my present predicament, I knew this would be the ultimate test. If I could get this group of homeless men to respond, anyone and everyone of sound mind could grasp the concept.

I put a plan together. First thing in the morning while Dom took the workers to the plant, I went shopping. Remembering what a clock had done for me, I bought 10 alarm clocks with the 2 bells on top and the little hammer in the middle. I also stopped by the bank and picked up a lot of singles. Dom and I set up times for each station. The team that drilled the 156 holes in the floor to install the seats and seatbelts needed 45 minutes, the team who put up the walls and ceiling needed 50 minutes. The carpet team needed 45 minutes and so on. Pretty soon we had 10 teams set up.

We taught each team exactly how to do their job and made them proficient at it. The next morning, we picked up the teams and headed out. On this day I tied the alarm clocks to the rearview mirror and called everyone outside. I stood up on a trailer and repeated these words: (Forgive my language) I held up about $500.00 in singles, $250.00 in each hand. As I waved the money in the air, I said, "Listen here you mother f----rs, you have an alarm clock in your van. All you have to do is beat the bell and do the job perfect and I will give you each $10 cash at that moment. Finish 10 vans today and beat the clock each time, and each member of your team can get $20.00

dollars extra. Beat the other team and you get an additional $5.

Holy shit, they took off like lightning. They worked like a well-oiled machine at high speed. Dom helped instruct the ones behind and made winners out of them consistently.

I spent time telling the guys what I had learned about success and some actually listened. I was in the midst of something I had wondered about for many years. Was this proof that anyone could decisively become dedicated?

How well did it go? On the day before everything was to be checked, this team, in the middle of the desert, in 95+ degree temperatures, built 17.5 vans and every one was perfect. Our warrantee was 3 years and we never had a call. 17.5 vans in one day, by a group of guys with a few days training; it still gives me chills. It always amazes me what a good man or woman can do in a day if they are single-minded and inclined to be productive.

But, there was also some magic. On day 5 a worker (Tommy) broke his hand. We rushed him into town and had it attended to. Tommy showed up with his hand all bandaged and said he wanted to go to work. In a hurry to get going I said "Tommy, I love you, but you are all fucked up." Tommy said, "Please, I will work with one hand so only pay me half." "I will pay you full, all you have to do is clean the floor all day, never let me see anything on the floor of the shop, jump in the truck." I felt like he needed to be with us. 2 days later Tommy kept trying to talk to me. I knew he was looking for money for his injured hand. That was fine, but I was on a mission and Dom and I had this program rolling, I would let nothing distract me. I kept pushing him off. The program was coming to an end and almost every van was complete and a handpicked team was putting a wrench or screwdriver on every screw and bolt. Final check, and everything had to be perfect. Tommy comes up to me and I said "Ok buddy, what's up?" he reached out his hand and grabbed mine and said, "I left home a few years ago. I have wanted to go back, but I felt worthless, this job changed my life. I am a man again and I went back home to my wife. You see, I went back a few times and stood outside in the dark, but I could not go in. Working here and being part of this changed me and gave me the confidence to go home, Sam, I want to thank you and Dom." He reached out and hugged me and we both cried.

The following year we were invited back to build more vans for the power plant. We called the homeless shelter to tell them we were coming and needed guys. I was wondering if some of our guys were still there, but I was hoping they made it out at the same time. About a week later I got a call. The man on the phone said, "I run a manufacturing plant in Phoenix and one of my workers is asking for 2 weeks off to come work with you. He said your job changed his life, is this bullshit or what?" I said, "Who is he?" He told me who the guy was, and I said, "I'd love to have him" and he was allowed to come work for us for 2 weeks.

As it turned out, he told Dom and I that being under that pressure that existed on the job site and hearing the positive things we told our workers, changed him. He married a girl from the homeless shelter and they both had jobs and an apartment. He said to me, "Sam, I just had to be part of this again."

In the end, everyone came to Dom or myself and thanked us for pushing them to give their all to the job. This was a great bunch of people and we loved every one of them and we learned they felt the same.

As for the task, well, we built 99 commuter conversion vans in the middle of the desert in 10 days. We learned later that other companies gave estimates of 6 weeks to build the same 99 vans at their plant. When I called my customer for the last payment, no one believed the vans were finished. They flew out from Detroit and were speechless. The inspector walked into every van, inspected them totally and called his boss and said, "Give this man a check. I don't know how they did it, but pay them."

Every one of us has greatness in us. Here were a group of men sleeping under tarps with nothing positive in their lives and they rose to the occasion and the occasion changed their life.

I believe human beings are capable of things greater than their soul, body, mind, learnings, capabilities and personality, provided they are working for a common good. As Aristotle said, "The sum is greater than the parts." It is like the Beatles. Individually they were ok, as a group they had tremendous impact on the music industry. I think those men chose to move forward in their quest through life, because they were determined to change things. They felt something they had lost, pride and achievement, they once again became motivated, and they liked it.

I asked myself many times, why did they put up with me? I yelled, I pushed, and demanded from them on an hourly and daily basis. I think that is the reason they stayed. They knew I had pride in them and I wanted more for them. I wanted to teach them how to earn more, and grow and gain back their confidence and will to succeed. I always thought they knew they were also teaching me something.

There were other projects around the country where we hired homeless people and the outcome was the same. Temporarily lost men, looking for a chance to prove themselves and find meaning in their lives again. In Seattle, we built 87 commuter vans for the city and all of them with homeless men. They were a tough group, a lot of real tough street men. Still, after 4 or 5 days they started to feel pride and rose to the occasion and Dom and I were proud to see how productive these men could be.

There was one guy in Seattle who once played for the Oakland Raiders. We hired him reluctantly and he did not like orders. He was just an ok worker and everyone else hated him. After about 5 days I said to Dom, "I am going to talk to him." I walked over to this giant of a man and looked up and said, "Hey, can I talk to you?", he grunted. I wanted to have a real heart to heart about his attitude and I figured if he is sitting down it would be easier to get away if it did not go well. "Have you noticed that everyone hates you?" There was no response. "Look, your life is none of my business, but I am guessing it sucks. Let's start off slow and see if we can change something. Just for the hell of it today, walk up to anyone in the shop and say, my name is Joe, what is yours and stick out your hand." He laughed at me in a smug kind of way. I thought I saw an opening so I said, "Don't worry if it does not go well, I will have your back." He cracked half a smile.

Dom and I stayed on him to tune up his work skills. He reached out to a few guys and within a week he was a popular, smiling fellow. In contrast, a week prior, he had laid claim to an old broken-down car. At bedtime, if you were sleeping in it, Joe would walk over and with one hand pick you up and drop you on the ground. But after our talk, he became part of the group.

Our shop was a very disciplined work place. It was run to finish a job well, and also offer the workers a chance to improve their lives and possibly learn something. In the morning, if you work for us, we start at 8 am. And you better be in the shop at 8am. At 8:01 you do not work for us. So, in the morning when we would come to work, there would be men sleeping in front of the front door. We could not get in unless we stepped on them. That usually did not happen on day one, but after they felt they were valuable to us, they became of value.

On the last days of this particular project, my partner Dom was noticeably tired. He'd been working outside in the hot sun and was getting dehydrated. I told Joe I need him to help me, he looked at me and said, "Sam, I can't, Dom is going to fall, he won't stop. He is dehydrated, I have seen it before on the field. If he falls I need to be there to catch him." He turned and ran across the street to work with Dom. He worked by Dom's side until they were finished. Here was a guy who had only been in it for himself just 20 days ago, and now he was more concerned about others than himself.

These men taught me that anyone can get up and change their circumstances or their behavior and it does not matter if you have been programmed by stories in a small kitchen in Italy or not. You can have it all, you just have to want it more than anything else.

Lucky for me I learned this before I got sick. Taking action to resolve my health problems is what I do. Every one of us can visualize themselves as healthy or successful and start on the road to recovery, or learn how to live as healthy as possible with whatever condition might be troubling you.

What is it that you want? Reduce it to a single goal. Want your health back? Just remember, you cannot go two places at once. One goal, one day at a time, and do not violate the one goal rule: See it in your mind's eye.

Our workers had a couple of nuts running around yelling and pushing them to keep that single-minded goal in front of them.

Many times, for me, it has been being able to stand in front of a mirror and saying to myself, "Ok, you are coming back, keep it up." And then I continue to exercise and eat smart and get my body ready to fight again.

I have learned through many battles, that succeeding is not as difficult as one might imagine.

Sitting down and writing a plan, starting it, and then staying on track is always the challenge. I believe for a plan to be successful, it needs to be a simple one. I think if your daily schedule once written, cannot fit on the back of a business card, it may be too complicated stay with.

When I am coming back from a setback in my health, I set up a schedule and put it on the back of a business card.

Up at 7am:
Run on odd days, 300 feet or 3 miles, just run what you can.

Breakfast:
Eggs with berry and vitamin drink.
lift weights even days.
Protein drink

Lunch:
protein and whole carbs.

Dinner:
fish, whole carbs
Bed time vegetable drink.

If I've lost a lot of weight, I include a calorie drink with protein. Some have as many as 530 calories and 22 grams of protein for just 8 ounces.

Coming back is a difficult time to stay on track. Dealing with all the pressures of being sick can easily be overwhelming. Aside from my health, there are usually business problems, and emotional problems, that in poor health, are magnified. A simple plan that I stick to strengthens me and helps me to move forward. I have used a recorder hooked up to a lamp timer as an alarm that helps me start the day off and reminds me to get up and reminds me that I must fight.

When I am really in bad shape because of loss of a weight and sickness my recorder will have a message to reassure me I can come back again,

"Good morning, today is another day to gain some ground. You are coming back. Get up and exercise and eat right. You are feeling stronger today. Meditate for a moment and visualize yourself being strong and productive and then get up and start todays fight."

It is always a battle when you are sick, on drugs or recovering from surgery, it is very hard to get on track. Keep your plan simple, write it out, use a recorded message, but rely on an outside goal and stick to it. It is all we have, an outside direction, contrary to how we feel.

CHAPTER 15
A HIGHER STANDARD

Things were coming together. I was now several years out from my last surgery, which cleaned up the adhesions, and I was putting my life back together again, piece by piece. We moved from our big beautiful house on Barnegat Bay, into a smaller older house in Warren, NJ. It was a great fit, as it was only 20 minutes from the office. Great property, but the house needed a lot of work.

I was working as hard as ever to regain our small fortune. I needed to find a balance of nutrition, exercise and work. This may be the most difficult thing I do from time to time. In my case, I do not have a colon and suffer occasionally from pouch itis. Basically, it has all the same symptoms of a good virus. When fighting constant dehydration, it interferes with my life, making it hard sometimes to be positive.

One day I was painting the lines on our tennis court and when I reached up to wipe away some sweat, I noticed a lump on my neck. I quickly went to a medical group and the head doctor assured me it was not cancer, yet every time he drained it, it came back. I finally drove up to the Lahey Clinic. There I ran into my dear friend, Dr. Coller (my colon rectal surgeon and friend). We talked and he said, "Sam, what is on your neck?" I told him, "That is why I am here". He said, "Sam, that could be cancer." You got to love the irony. Here I am seeing 2 specialists in head and neck cancer who took biopsies (the wrong kind I found out) and here is a colon rectal surgeon who pin points it in 2 minutes. After the tests, it turned out to be cancer again. Dr. Dolan from the Lahey Clinic did the biopsy. While home waiting for the biopsy report, I plan how I will handle it.

What to do:

The good news is I have spent years indicating to my family and friends to hold me to my standards. There are two types of family and friends and I love them both. There are the ones that I know I cannot fail because they need me. Then there are the others who are just waiting for me to fall, and of course I do not want to give them the satisfaction. Regardless, it is pressure, good pressure to win again.

For the most part, it is about having a lot to live up to. I have spent my life helping my wife and daughter see the benefits of sometimes having to fight and struggle. My little girl, (not so little any longer) and wife have seen me fight back several times from 130 pounds and almost financially bankrupt a few times. They both have developed the same principles. People who know me often ask, how I do it? How do I keep my businesses and property and keep opening new ones with all my health problems?

The answer is very simple, I HAVE NO CHOICE.

Remember, I was raised, along with my sister, who is a rock herself, by a wonderful, tough, man, my dad. After my mom died, he gave up his every moment to be with us and raise us, putting his dreams and wants aside.

And then there is my wife, she has had to drag me from hospital to hospital for years, through one cancer after another, bone disease and back to fighting another cancer and always she is there for me. This has gone on for 36 years. She was with me when we made millions and built a grand home on Barnegat Bay and then lost it all to another cancer and then built it all back again, only to fall to another cancer and major loss again.

I tell a funny story amongst friends of my wife and I how, when I had my first cancer, she was there when I went from 180 to 125 pounds. Fighting to stay here, she was with me, when I had multiple smaller surgeries and one 12 hour surgery. When I had several other small diseases, she was there, when I had a debilitating bone disease, she stood by my side. When I contracted head and neck cancer, she was there and on and on. Some say what a wonderful woman; on the other hand, I wonder if she is just bad luck!

Then there is my little girl, so many battles she has fought through to victory. I thank God that she had the opportunity to watch me fight through life, it has ingrained within her, the spirit to fight and never give up. Like the time the private school she was attending said, at the age of 7, she had to leave the school. They said she will never keep up as she has a severe reading problem. I made her come to that meeting against the school's counselors wishes. She sat and listened as they explained that she belongs in a public school where they can handle her problem. She sat and listened and then I held her hand and I explained to her as best I could.

"Honey, they are saying you have a reading problem and they want you to leave the school, leave all your friends and start over in a strange place where you will have to make all new friends."

She looked at me. Then I said, "So here are your options, we can run from this school and go and start over or we can stay and fight and beat them and show them you belong here. So, what do you want to do?"

A very uncomfortable few moments went by while she was thinking and then she looked at me and said.

"Let's beat them, Daddy."

My wife and I and Samantha went to work and I guess I can best explain how she did by telling you this.

Our little 7 year old girl had decided she was staying with her friends and at her school and worked tirelessly to learn how to read and comprehend. My wife worked with her and I had the privilege of working with her every night. And on those nights, we read and read and one day she looked up at me and said these words.

"You know what, Daddy?"

"What, honey?"

"Reading is always going to be special to me because I had to earn it and all the other little boys and girls can just do it"

Then she looked down and kept reading her story.

11 years later she graduated with her class from that school and went on to attend Boston University.

At the beginning of her senior year of high school we went to my daughter's school for their Convocation. The entire student body was there with family and faculty. The headmaster called on one person he singled out as being worthy of reading a very important inspirational message to all. Samantha stood up and walked up to the podium and stood there so proud, and did an unbelievable job.

Sometimes in life, you win big.

I am being held to a higher standard of performance by the achievements and dedication of those I love.

I started thinking about the process of recovery and pity. So now the question came up: Where am I really at? How bad am I? Am I lying down because I was taught to lie down, am I capable of more? Am I sick or is my body sick. Is it time to separate them so I can go forward?   Could my state of mind, my pain, be a product of what I was taught, or a result of my present health situation?

My doctors and family urge me to rest and take it easy, are they right? Or are they part of the problem that is our society? I know one thing, there is a rule that cannot be denied "the more you do today, the more you can do tomorrow and the less you do today, the less you can do tomorrow".

The confusing part for me is, how do you know when you are ready? I observe Mother Nature and how quickly it reclaims its mistakes, how fast things recover that were devastated. While thinking about the animal kingdom, which is full of further examples of rapid recovery, I remembered my dog and how quickly he recovered from surgery.

Here is how I handle things that happen to me. When I feel sorry for myself and want to lie down because I am tired, I think of who I am responsible to and I remember two things that I have observed in my life:

1. Thinking of my dog, I ask my wife to go to the pet store and get a collar for me and push me out the door and let me go to work. Lucky for me my wife knows I am a little nuts and humors me.

2. Remember the story I told you about the two girls who wanted to come over my house the night I was deathly sick. If I can rise to the occasion for a night of sex with two lovely young ladies, it is clear, I must second guess myself every time I feel like taking it easy because I am sick.

I know it is hard to separate being human from what you are told you need, but I also know life is simple, so keep it simple. If quitting was natural, we would not be here.

Waiting for the results of a cancer test is an interesting time for me. It always brings me close to the most important things in life, family and friends. On this particular sunny day, I am working in the backyard and sitting on my tractor looking at what I have to live for. Since all these illnesses started at the age of 29, I pretty much thank God for every day and I really try not to forget the gift of a day. While sitting all the way to the rear of my property, I find myself laughing and thinking to myself "Why me? It is just another battle. I have to fight and kick its ass." I tell myself this while looking across my tennis court, up a hill to a small green house, (where I grow tomatoes) across the lawn to the pool area and a 110 foot water slide.

This is our special backyard. When my daughter was about 8, she and I would go on the computer, night after night and look for someone selling a back-yard water slide for the pool. One day I came across an amusement park in Florida closing. It seemed they had two water slides that were 265 feet long. Right off the bat we knew we had something. Samantha and I looked at each other. "Dad, that is cool." "It sure is" I agreed. "Dad, there is no way we can tell mom", She said, "Not until it gets here, anyway", I told her.

I made a deal with her, I said, "Honey, if we get the slide, we cannot go to Disney World for 7 years." (we usually stopped on the way to our home in Florida) "No problem Dad, I will have Disney World right here."

I worked out a deal with the amusement park in Florida who owned one of the slides, the pump, the poles that hold it up and all the bolts and extra pieces. I found a company to truck it, guys to disassemble it and load it. Soon, it was on its way in a 56 foot tractor trailer. It arrived at my shop one day and we unloaded it. My most vivid memory of that day was after we unloaded it onto the 4000 sq. ft. floor, my partner Dom, looked at me and said. "What the hell did you get me into now?" He knew he would be helping me.

Dom and I erected this monster in the back of my house. We only put up 110 feet, it was something to see. I planted large ever greens all around to keep it somewhat concealed.

It is a special place. I have a great life, filled with trials in both business and health, but what a gift, the right to fight every day of my life.

However, for now, it seems like I am jumping back on the medical merry go round, that is a very familiar place to me, round and round I go, grabbing for that brass ring, all the while hoping and striving for the conductor to let me off. You have to wait for a clearing and jump back into your life. I know the question that haunts me is, when to jump. Make your move too soon and you might hit the wall, land on an innocent bystander or worse yet, impale yourself on the brass ring dispenser.

And then there are the motivations to make the right choice and heal. Staying alive has new meaning again, my little girl. I knew I had to stay alive as long as possible to protect my family. I find myself very engrossed with the thought of my wife and my daughter being alone if I make the wrong decision. With my experimental pouch and other issues all handled previously at the Lahey Clinic, I knew I had to be there. Back up to the Lahey Clinic where Dr. Dolan removed the lymph node in my neck. Then on to Radiation with Dr. Garren.

It was clear that if anyone would have a worst-case scenario, it would be me. Dr. Garren and I thought it was a good idea to go for a more aggressive amount of radiation. Too little and there are no second chances.

I had to move to Burlington, Mass. as the treatments were every day, twice a day for 7 weeks. Then a strange thing happened, a doctor at the clinic offered to have me stay with him and his family during the treatment. I am a very private person and at first I thought it was crazy. As it turned out, I took him up on it for about 4 weeks and then I was feeling so poorly from the radiation, I needed to be in a place of my own, so I moved into a local hotel.

I finished my radiation and it really kicked my ass. I lost weight, infections in my throat caused my pouch to become infected and basically, I went in and out of the hospital for months. Then home on feeding tubes and back to the hospital with another infection.

At this point I am a fraction of me. Trying to keep the one vision in front of me, that it is not about me, it is about getting healthy again so I can protect and build for those I love. In time, I got stronger. Eating was very difficult as the passage way in my throat was small and the throat muscles were damaged from the radiation.

I was working again and interacting with life. I talked a little funny, but I was moving forward. Every restaurant we went to knew me and when we came in they would set me up with 4 large glasses of water. The radiation had decimated my saliva glands. A bowl of angel hair pasta (one of the easier things to eat) takes about 2 quarts of water.

Talking is difficult and I suffer from constant throat infections that devastate my pouch, but I am learning to handle that. Can't say enough about colloidal silver for sinus and throat infections.

My life has again become more complicated, but I have a life again. I am working out and I feel good about the future. I have adjusted to all the special requirements and most of the world sees me as a normal guy.

During the years of putting my life back together after my last cancer, there were many ups and downs when my health went to hell and I lost 15 or so pounds from throat and pouch infections in a few days, but all and all, that is just part of my new life.

There is something special about planning your day and having a good day you earned, you own it. Every day belongs to you, you worked for it, you designed it and you prepared for it. I am not rushing through life, I am feeling every moment.

I rely on my vision of another tomorrow to keep me motivated. Usually that vision is on a small card I carry when I am in trouble, a vision of a place to get to.

When I was a young man I wanted to have one million dollars before the age of 30. I knew I had some real battles ahead. Maybe the biggest one was that I hated to get up early in the morning. I tried everything to handle this problem.

One day I drove out to Radio Shack on Rt. 22 In Union, NJ in my 1967 Pontiac Lemans. I found a timer to turn lights on and off so crooks would think I was home and I also bought a cassette tape recorder. I went home and set it up so the timer started the cassette recorder at 6am. Next, I recorded a message. It went like this. *"Good morning Sam, it is 6 am and you have to get up and go achieve your goal. I know you feel like staying in bed, but you need to get out. Remember that English tudor house, the family and life you always dreamed of, well get up and go get it. Time to get up: Get up! You are killing your dreams and you will end up with nothing in life! Let's get up, be full of energy and positive and become successful."* At that point if I have not gotten out of bed, it speaks to me in language I really understand. *"Hey, you lazy piece of shit, you fucking bum, you are going to have nothing! You are going to be living a shit life! Get your fucking ass out of that bed and get going."*

There were mornings when I had failed to get up during the positive portion. However, without question I always got up. Sometimes I started my day pissed off, but I was up.

As a young man I read something that stuck with me. "The first hour of the morning is the rudder of the day." Keep that in mind and start your day in the direction you want it to go.

Of course, I have battles with myself while sitting on the edge of my bed: I am weak today. I should sleep late. I better not get up early. My throat is hurting. I woke up 6 times last night and it took me a long time to fall back to sleep.

There is only one way to beat that. I have a daily list of what I need to do. The recorder that wakes me up to my simple goal, or a piece of paper the size of a business card with my single goal on it, helps me visualize while I meditate on achieving my specific goals. No truer words were ever said than, "The first hour of the morning is the rudder of the day." If I take the few moments before I fall asleep and when I wake in the morning to re-set my goal fresh in my mind, it is always a better day. Truth be told, I still need a note to motivate me to exercise because I still do not like it. I always feel better when it is over, so you would think the positive result would make me look forward to it, but you would be wrong.

So, keep in mind that there will be days you will not want to do the things on your list or on your note card, but remember, if you do tackle them, you will feel better, you will feel a sense of accomplishment because you have owned another day.

CHAPTER 16 LOOKING HARD

On October 6, 2015, I woke up with a tongue that seemed swollen. I have had a lot of trouble after the radiation with infections of the mouth and throat, so I chalked it up to a new infection. Thinking I will jump into my routine of colloidal silver spray every 30 minutes, 50/50 mixture of water and hydrogen peroxide gargle, increase my turmeric, limit my diet and in a few days I will have it under control. As the day progressed it got worse. The next morning it was more difficult to talk and swallow. I called my local doctor and he sent me to another doctor. That doctor said my tongue was swollen and he gave me prednisone. It seemed to lessen the swelling or the anxiety, but not by much. Swallowing was very difficult, even water was tough. Three days later and still dealing with the swollen tongue, I felt very weak and fell to the floor in my office. As I lay there, I started going through every moment of the last several days. It became clear to me that I had not altered my work schedule in spite of my new health problem. The separation of body and mind that has given me such a full life, now caused me to overlook a serious problem. I take excellent care of my body, but I fight to keep it away from me. It tends to be a pain in the ass. This time, my separation caught up with me.

Laying on the floor, very lightheaded, I traced my last several days. I realized I had not kept up with the amount of water it takes to keep me going because of the new difficulty in swallowing. Not having a colon (lost it in 1984) it is difficult to absorb water from food or drink. I realized I needed to stay on the floor for a while and drink, as I was pretty sure I was dehydrated. Staying hydrated at my work pace with the pouch and the radiation damage to my throat is always a challenge, but I manage. However, this time it was different. While I was on the floor drinking and resting, I noticed I could not see out of my left eye. As I concentrated, I noticed it was only the bottom 50% that seemed to be dark.

Constantly drinking and resting, I felt stronger in about 3 hours. I was no longer dizzy and felt better. I drove home and rested and my wife made an appointment with my eye doctor. Soon we discovered that the eye had damage due to lack of blood supply and lost vision. They called it an ocular stroke. Luckily it was not connected to a stroke.

It was time to get up to the Lahey Clinic and see my doctors. My first doctor was my ENT,   Dr. Dolan. I told him the doctors were treating me for a swollen tongue. He looked at my tongue and in two seconds said, "Sam, your tongue is not swollen." I argued and he explained that he thought it was nerve damage. He was familiar with the radiation I had on my head and neck and thought it might be that.

Off to the nerve doctors and ultimately, they admitted me for a raft of tests for, stroke, heart attack, blood clots, nerve damage and on and on. Soon we made an educated guess that the tongue was not related to the eye and the tongue was the beginning of ALS or nerve damage from the radiation, which would continue.

The diagnosis was too early to tell which way I was going and what nerve disease it might be. Back home I tried to get my life back on track. Eating of course proved to be nearly impossible. My throat had been damaged from the radiation, which caused a narrowing and deformity of my throat and the reduction of saliva glands made eating very difficult. At home I can manage through a meal of non-connective tissue food by choking and coughing, hoping it may level out. I cook most of our meals, so I can tailor them.

As time passes, I find an elusive balance to be the norm. Different again and a little more demanding, but I am working and aside from doing a great impression of Elmer Fudd whenever I talk, I continue going forward.

Long nights are not new to me, but more complicated. The lack of tongue control causes excessive drying of the mouth, as it has somehow redirected the one saliva gland to send saliva down my throat, which aspirates into my lungs.

Keeping busy is so important. I started building proto types of some ideas that I have had for years. The middle of the night, I stand in my home shop, surrounded by welders, drill press, lath, wood planer, table saw, radial arm saw, band saw, 6 foot rolling tool box filled with every hand tool, 2 work benches, grinders, buffers, air compressor, lumber, sheet metal, raw steel and all the hand tools from my days as a body man, as well as my construction equipment. It is a great place to be distracted from my body's reality.

Yes, I spend more time alone, but I really enjoy working alone. On good nights, none of my shortcomings rear their ugly heads. I have filed a few patents and am currently building another proto type. One in the food industry which I licensed to a company, you can see it at **https://www.finediningchafer.com/;** one is in the security business, which I manufactured, you can see it at **https://www.latchcatch.com/.** I am currently selling the third patent to the pleasure industry and finishing designs on the fourth patent also in the food industry.

It is so important to be doing something positive. It doesn't matter if it works, as long as it is positive and for a greater goal.

When I asked recently if my tongue will function as it once did, I was told "Once nerves disconnect, they do not reconnect. If they did, millions of people who are in wheel chairs would stand up and walk, it just does not happen." I know they are right, but I also know I was in 4th degree collapse of the right femur and no one recovers from that. That was 1986 and I still have my femur.

I have had the good fortune to be taught by my hero in life, my dad, now 99 years old. He taught me to keep getting up. When I was young he said this to me, "Chop, if he knocks you down, get up, and if he knocks you down again, get up, and keep getting up. You may not win the fight, but never quit fighting." Great advice from a great man. It has served me well.

Off I go into another battle. During the course of all of this I have been taking stock of what has worked for me and what is just hype or misguided information.

The Doctor: It is so clear to me that you need a doctor who has dealt with a lot of situations. Experience really is important. If your doctor tells you nutrition and exercise are not a factor, move on. My first great doctor and a leader in his field, Dr. Coller, was at the Lahey Clinic back in 1983. We sat and I asked a lot of questions I had about nutrition. He said "Sam, never make the mistake of consulting with a doctor about nutrition unless he is known for his nutritional approach. I have had 8 years of medical training and 8 hours of nutritional training." A lesson well heard.

Recently, my closest friend had prostate cancer. He had been treated 14 years ago with seeds, but it was back. He was banged around from doctor to doctor and one day he asked me to get involved. Together we met with a few doctors. It was clear that everyone was going to radiate the lymph gland on the left, but something was bothering me. I finally got the tests and after sitting with several qualified people, something started to rear its ugly head.

Every doctor was radiating the left enlarged lymph gland, however the right one was also enlarged. You could argue that it is a little smaller, but it was not a good argument. Every institution was radiating just one. This includes the largest cancer institutes in the USA. I sat with my friend and asked him to pick a facility he wanted to go to and make an appointment with the doctor for the three of us to talk.

The day came and we sat with the doctor. He was qualified, had the right radiation equipment, but we had one issue. I said, "Thanks for taking the time to meet with us. I would like to talk about Dom's treatment and all I ask is that you keep an open mind to my objective, which is keeping Dom alive as long as possible." He looked at me funny, but he acknowledged that we had an agreement. "I know that this is a business and it has to make money, I also know that very often businesses have to make decisions and those decisions are made by business men and not doctors. Doctors may disagree, but between keeping the facility open to be of service to the community and making a profit, it gets blurry." I could see in his eyes he knew I understood the bottom line. I continued. "In Dom's case, there is a clear necessity to radiate both the right and left lymph node at the same time. I understand that the insurance companies only pay for the treatment regardless if there are 1 or 4 targets. So, by just radiating one node now and in another few months radiating the other one, the hospital will make twice the money plus more visits. Meanwhile Dom is at a much higher risk." He looked at me for a moment and said, "I was not aware there were two nodes enlarged." I handed him the pictures of the nodes and he said, "I see what you are referring to, let me look this over and I am sure we can accommodate Dom's request to radiate both at the same time." I thanked him and then he said, "You are right, the decisions are no longer made by the doctors, it is business and profits."

When I sat with my friend with prostate cancer and his doctor at the cancer hospital he chose, I asked the hard questions. Doc, what are the numbers here. With the position Dom is in: How long will he live? How will he live? What is the long-term prognosis and I am not talking about a 5-year success rate? I want the real projection based on everything you know and the clinical history of his condition. He talked and it was followed by more questions. The goal is to get a vision of what happens and then improve on it, you have to have something to beat. By the way, the hospital agreed to radiate both together and so far, so good.

My father-in-law was in the hospital and the doctors had scheduled him for open heart surgery. He had several heart attacks and strokes and was frail. I was very concerned that he would not survive the procedure. I discussed using the excimer laser instead of surgery, however the doctors assured me it was not an option. They insisted surgery was the best thing. My father-in-law consented to letting me get involved. I commandeered a copy of the tests and sent them to the doctor who invented the excimer laser. He assured me that the laser could be used for the procedure my father-in-law needed, but said in his condition he recommended doing nothing. I consulted with another doctor who also said, "Do nothing."

I set up an appointment with the doctors who were readying my father in law for transport to another hospital for surgery. I presented the facts and information. One doctor looked at the other and said, "Mr. Casternovia, we have discussed this and we agree, it would be best for your father-in-law to go home and manage the condition with drugs." Luckily, he lived for many years.

Be a family that is informed. Getting informed and helping your doctor help you is the best path. Let him know you are participating; he will appreciate it. For me, I am working with some great people and all the time looking for outside info that may change my life for the better.

The funny thing about where I am at this point in my life, I have learned to get out of my body's problems and go forward, so much so that regularly I will wake in the morning and cook my breakfast, shower, dress and go to work as a normal person, but with a lot of water to get my food down. Then comes the inevitable first meeting with someone, maybe it is just getting gas or at one of my attorney's offices or the bank, and I go to talk. So, try as I may, it is very hard to speak clearly. The first thing that happens is I find it very funny. Actually, it is a surprise to me that I can't talk normally. Just proof I am doing my job and leaving that pain in the ass body out of my life.

There are some very smart doctors who have small practices, who can help you work through problems. I have a doctor in my home town, Dr. Clemente, who I rely on. He is smart and never shoots from the hip or passes you off. He listens and looks into your concerns and options and shares them with you. The right local doctor can help you find the right place to go to seek treatment, but remember, it is your health and you must find the best path for your treatment and recovery. Once you find the treatment you need, search for the best place to have it. Ask questions and continue to ask questions until you really understand where you are going with your health.

CHAPTER 17
BELIEVING

I am fond of life and consider my life a great gift, to me. I am a God fearing man with a deep responsibility for the gift I have been given. I am not qualified to advise anyone on religion, but I will tell you this, find one. When you do, or if you were brought up in a religious belief and it suggests that all other religions and people should be condemned, well, get out and find a better one. I guarantee, any religion that teaches hate, will severely limit, if not make happiness impossible. Additionally, it seems being old, or sick, is much easier with a belief in a higher power. My faith in God has been a real blessing for me and a source of great comfort in times of stress, illness and pain. My responsibility to reach out to family, friends and those who are about to become my friends is a great comfort and gives me purpose, all of which help minimize my situation. You will not find me in a church every Sunday, but daily, I pray to God and Jesus with great pleasure and feel a deep connection.

When my daughter was young I held tight to the Santa Clause belief. People said to me, "She still believes in Santa?" The answer was profoundly, yes. I wanted her to learn as a very young person that a strong belief and visualization of a joyous day was to come true. It is clear to any person who is single-mindedly focused on one thing, stay focused and it becomes reality. Yes, it requires effort and work, but work without belief, seldom brings you closer to your goal. Without limiting yourself to one vision and a self-imposed mindset, little happens to reach your goal, no matter how hard you work. Don't believe me, just look at the guy digging a ditch, all day, throwing dirt over his head, sweating and gasping for a breath and at the end of the day he gets a self-sustaining pay check, his vision. He needed a vision to get to the next level, a belief in something beyond the moment of just digging that ditch. No one works harder than him and true to the natural order of life, he secures his vision, a pay check. So, for my daughter, Santa was the first step to believing in something you could not see or touch, but it happened, because she believed. I knew she did not have to understand it, but I also knew it would stay with her.

When I was young and searching for my path to obtain the 5 riches of life: 1. Emotional: to be able to sit in a room alone and like myself for who I have become, 2. Spiritual: to connect with a higher force and feel connected, 3. Social: to have the right kind of friends who are making a difference in the life around them, 4. Health: to take what has been given me and be responsible for making it all it can be, 5. Financial: to be financially stable to care for those I love and protect them. I read stories of successful men and after a while, it was pretty clear that there were truths missing. I knew from what I had experienced with my probes into people's lives that IQ and education were important, but I knew a lot of educated people whose life was not anything I looked up to or wanted. The notion that all men are created equal, well, I have a real tough time with that one. Just look around, if I was to think I could run with the fastest of runners or play any sport professionally or discus quantum physics (no matter how much training I had) I would be delusional at best. I know who I am.

On the other hand, we are equal in our ability to achieve greatness. I learned something about people and success. It does not matter what your education level is. You do not have to believe that God set the natural order forth as I do, but you cannot deny the natural order of things. Be it God or evolution that cultivated the natural order, it exists. And as I said before, the natural order does not care whether your goal is positive or negative, it will bring you to it, provided you follow the rules of engagement. Likewise, it stands to reason that success in life, will not only be for the very intelligent or gifted or the highly educated. Evolution of our culture and our history has proven that, just by the fact that we are still here.

So as a young man looking for answers before I started my quest, I looked at the animal kingdom. You have heard all the stories about a family on vacation and their dog or cat gets lost hundreds of miles from home, only to show up at their door step 6 months later. Or the fact that a homing pigeon can travel thousands of miles (longest flight 7200 miles) to find his way home from a place he has never been before.

It stands to reason that we have some ability to reach our goals equally. However, we are back to that one thing, a single-minded vision. The lost animal or homing pigeon were not thinking of anything else but home. That vision remained etched into their minds. Reason tells me, that my victories were not so great, I was just using the natural order of things. What was different was that I followed the rules. Remember them, the two rules that pretty much cover everything: #1. As long as you are doing what you feel like doing, you will never have what you want. It is reasonable to assume that the pigeon and lost animals would have felt like laying down and not fighting to get home, but instead they took the hard and tough road to get to where they wanted to be. Rule # 2. You become what you think about all day long. For sure these animals only had one vision before them, HOME. A clear picture of their life at HOME. From then on, they were driven to their goal by the natural order of things.

I have had many people in my life ask me about reaching their own goal. First thing I do is ask them to cover their eyes and tell me what they see. I tell them the facts, if your goal is not your 24-hour 7 day a week vision that haunts your every moment, it will not happen, period.

Don't let me over simplify winning, it is hard to keep your vision with you every moment. And of course, it is challenging to reach any goal worthwhile. However, it is always worth the effort to live healthier with your situation or live financially secure. Always better to keep fighting.

Never forget that it is your problem, be it your health or finances. You are in this battle to discover the best options to reach that goal. A well-informed patient gets better care from his doctor. By the same token, a well-educated business man attracts better options. It is all about hard work and a single-minded vision.

Of course, there are pitfalls and obstacles in life. For me, I have questioned my constant battle with illnesses. I learned years ago to get past my questioning of why and focus on how to beat it. So, I have set my mind in somewhat of a reality-based vision, the reality of what I know I want and do not have at the moment.

My latest gift seems to be radiation, the gift that keeps on giving. It has damaged my nerves, muscles etc. in my neck, so I have now suffered debilitating cramping and pain just trying to hold my head up. Trying to solve this new mystery I decided to attack it with the same exercises that a professional wrestler uses for his neck. First, I bought a head harness to fasten to weights to strengthen my neck. Well, it was of little use. As the months passed, ability to hold my head up without pain mounted. I finally bought a $1,000.00 wrestler's neck exercising machine (but for only $125). Within 8 weeks, my neck was stronger and most of the pain was gone. It literally changed my life. When I went away for 3 weeks without the machine, my neck started hurting. For me, it has helped improve things tremendously.

Compliments come from strange circumstances. There are two doctors that specialize in my syndrome. One is out of the USA and another is 10 miles from my office (lucky me). I went to see him and we talked for about an hour. He smiled from time to time and then he said, "Sam, I am the foremost authority on your syndrome. I have been seeing patients and studying it for 20+ years. After reading your file, I expected to see a very disabled man, you are the healthiest sick man I have ever seen, keep doing what you are doing."

Dealing with new obstacles is always challenging no matter how big or small. I look at it this way, God has so many diseases. He cannot prevent them, so he tries to give them to those of us who may have a better time dealing with them. Why else would my life have been so filled with health problems and then side effects from the treatment of the original disease?

I imagine God saying, "Who can we give this to?"

An angel says, "How about, Sam?"

God says, "Sam, isn't he here yet?"

"No, he made it through the last 4."

"Are you sure?"

"Yes, it says so right here, (as God's helper points to a computer filled with names) He is still working, actually, he is working 6 days a week 10 to 12 hours a day."

God, looks over the notes in the computer and sees that I am still fighting and in the process of putting up a warehouse and a 6 family house, along with 3 new patents filed. He notices that I have cared for those close to me and others I do not know.

"God, it says here that Sam has thanked you many times for his first cancer. He said it gave him the time to educate himself, making up for his misspent youth. He credits your gift of his first cancer as the driving force for his success, family, friends, education, wisdom and all that is important to him."

"Well, it seems like I made a pretty good choice to send him those diseases." God states.

"God, Sam has said many times; I am a better man sick, than I ever was healthy."

A moment of silence and God says

"OK, send it to Sam."

Sounds crazy, but it works for me.

I have come to believe that we are a very small part of what or who we really are. We seldom let who we are meant to become, rise to fruition. Our presence is not singular, we are being beckoned to let the good that is around and in us, become part of who we are and change the world around us, for the better. Unfortunately, our prejudices and ill guided teachings often fight off the good we are destined for and lead us to mediocrity. How many times I have heard people say, "I know what is best for me," and yet they sit in a position of stagnation, want and quiet anger, never really enjoying the life gifted to them. They lean towards the promises of others vying for their favor, offering promises that never come, and yet they support those who promise, in spite of receiving nothing.

Life is full of pitfalls and opportunities. In times of peril it can be difficult to see the opportunities around us, but they are there. We must always remember that knowledge, true knowledge will enlighten us.

One of my favorite stories is the guy who is on the roof of his house and the flood waters are rising. A boat with rescued people clinging to the rails pulls up and urges him to jump in; he says, "Go my friend, God will save me." Shortly thereafter a helicopter arrives and lowers a rope, he waves them off, and shouts, "God will save me," and refuses the rope ladder. Soon the water rises and sweeps him off the roof and he dies. He arrives up in heaven and the first thing he says to God is, "God, why didn't you save me?" "God looks at him and says, I sent you a boat and a helicopter, what do you want from me?"

Everything is in our hands, we have the power, the ability to accomplish our goals regardless of what they are. Our health, how we live with sickness, how we live in general, how we treat others, how others treat us, how your family lives and benefits from the kind of person you are. We just must be responsible.

The great privilege I had wrapped up in an old blanket, in the corner of that cold damp basement watching my hero fight for his loved ones and his goals, lives in my heart every day, but what happened after great effort and sacrifice in that room, when those machines started to work again, was not of earthly origin.

That night, and so many other times in my life, the natural order of life was visible. Dad honored it by working and fighting for a single goal, to get his business of coin operated laundry equipment back on track. The effort and respect he showed was magnified 10-fold in both our lives. You cannot touch it or see it, but you sure can feel it. It is only visible to those that take the hard road, those who are willing to never surrender when things get tough.

I have seen unexplainable forces working and all have an origin of belief, hard work and a strong, single-minded focus. To this day, I wonder about things that have happened in my life. How did I end up living in the perfect knotty pine, top floor bedroom, once owned by my friends? The same house that I had so many dreams about and wished so hard to be mine for so long, I can't answer that, but there have been so many of those incidents in my life that are similar. There are forces at work for us, we just have to be aware of them and be receptive to their help.

The natural order of life does not care, it will equally reward you with good or bad. You are the gate keeper of your mind, guard it well, and fill it with a positive vision.

My time on the mountain in a snow storm has always been a source of guidance for me. The fact is, I knew I was on the right path heading towards my car and safety, yet I doubted myself and turned around. Had a man not come along and rescued Duchess and myself, well I don't think I would be writing this. I am going to admit that day set in motion a mindset, that to this day, haunts me. You see, I never, ever turn around on a goal that I have researched and set in front of me. The bad news is, there have been times I should have abandoned projects or paths as they failed, the good news is there were a lot more wins. You do not have to win a lot to have a lot. Set your goal and never turn around.

There is always time to do a project or reach a goal, you simply need to make the time and take advantage of the time you have. Don't be afraid to put pressure on yourself to succeed. When I found that time clock, it started a pattern in my life that everyone either admired or made fun of. When I worked in the body shop, they called me the streaker because I ran every place I went. Set demands for yourself and you will grow. Do not be disappointed if you fail, you will win another time, but never stop pushing forward.

Remember what Mark Twain said, "I am an old man and have known a great many troubles, most of which have never happened." We get lost in our problems and allow them to fester.

Late at night when I am alone thinking about my life, it is clear to me that my greatest motivation is responsibility to my gifts and those I love. I do not have the right to lay down and stop fighting. I am responsible to those who love me and I love as well. I think about my life in the terms of, "did I make a difference"?

Several years ago, when my daughter went off to college, I was cleaning up and I came across this:

Through a window I see my father, as I have countless times before, only this time it's different. Instead of looking out and seeing him leaving early in the morning for work, or completing a project in the back yard, he lies on a bed, in a white room, with tubes in his arms. I remain outside looking in, wondering why this happened again.

My father had his first cancer, colon cancer, before I was born. For as long as I can remember my father has referred to this tragedy as God's greatest gift to him. This forced him to reevaluate and rebuild his life for the better. Since I could talk, my father instilled three lessons into me: (1) doing what you feel like doing in life keeps you where you are; knowledge, perseverance, and a plan will bring you success; (2) you become what you think about all day long; and (3) every day is a gift. Regardless of how many times my father recited these words to me, I never truly understood them. Then, in June of 2008, at the end of seventh grade, my father was diagnosed with his second cancer, head and neck cancer. This time the life changing revelation was mine, and I know that its occurrence, along with my father's parenting, shaped my life tremendously over the last four years.

From my early childhood, my parents began to prepare me for the possibility of my father's illness returning and his possible death. Not wanting my first funeral to be my father's, my parents began to take me to the funerals of friends and family. Having attended 23 funerals thus far, I think we can say with confidence, mission accomplished. Though I always knew the return of cancer in my father was inevitable, when it actually happened, it seemed surreal.

It forced me to reevaluate my own, quiet, sit in the back of the class room and let life fly by existence. That year I did a lot of thinking about my life. If something happened to me, what had I done with my time? With this thought running through my mind, I determined that the most important things in my life were my family and friends.

Once my eighth-grade year started, I clung to the things that were familiar and gave my life the most stability: school and yearbook. As those first few weeks went by, I began to care less about what others thought of me and more about what I thought of myself. I took my father's first lesson and applied it to my schoolwork, raising my grades while my parents were in another state seeking treatment for him. I also accepted a higher position on the yearbook staff. I then took my father's next lesson and decided to make myself more positive. Though others had always considered me a happy girl, my own concerns often cluttered my head. I took it upon myself to reorganize my priorities.

Entering high school, I laid out a four year plan to become editor-in-chief of the yearbook and to acquire an internship working with Dr. Joshua Garren at the Lahey Clinic. Along the way I earned an editor position on the school newspaper and a spot on a varsity athletic team. I then focused on my father's last lesson, and I still strive to remember it every day. I know that no matter what life brings, each day is a gift. Still having my father with me makes every day even more precious.

Maybe, just maybe, I am making a difference. Thank you, God, for my life, family and friends.

My journey forward in life or when I am coming back from an illness, always brings me back to my roots, these two simple rules I discovered as a young man:

1. You become what you think about all day long. The thought or vision of yourself you harbor in your heart and mind at any given time, will be your destiny. We must guard the gate of our mind against negative information.

2. As long as you are doing what you feel like doing, you will never have and or become what you want. I always have to act against my current feelings to grow.

I hope my life experiences will add to your life.

Your opinion of my book is important to me, it helps me become a better writer. Would you please go back to Amazon and leave a review? I read all the reviews. My next book THE PIECE is a work in progress and your reviews will help me make it better.

Thank you
Sam

Made in the USA
Middletown, DE
29 July 2019